How We Built Our Dream Practice

Innovative Ideas for Building Yours

Dave Verhaagen Ph.D. and Frank Gaskill Ph.D.

Published by TPI Press, The Practice Institute, LLC, Camp Hill, PA 17011
All rights reserved. Published 2014.
Printed in the United States of America

ISBN: 0990344509
ISBN 13: 9780990344506
Library of Congress Control Number: 2014944126
Published by TPI Press, The Practice Institute, LLC,
Camp Hill, PA

To Ellen, my partner in life and craziness. "You can't make this stuff up!"
To Pam Abraham, who influenced me professionally more than she knows.
To Todd Williams, my best friend and one of the
greatest humans on the planet.
—Dave

To Liz, you took the biggest risk when we moved back to North Carolina.
Thank you for believing in me and giving me the chance to
create my dream practice. I love you.
Thank you to my lifelong friend and mentor, Dave Verhaagen. Whether
you will own this or not, I'm a psychologist because of you.
And finally, to the staff of Southeast Psych, a family that will be here
long after we are gone. Thank you for making this the
most funnest place ever!
—Frank

Contents

Introduction

We were in Orlando for the American Psychological Association's national convention with a bunch of the Southeast Psych staff. One evening, we had booked a reservation for a big table at a restaurant in town called Café Tu Tu Tango. We had no idea what to expect. What we got was something memorable and remarkable. Not only was the food unique and outstanding, but the experience was unlike any other restaurant. Within a few minutes of being seated, an African drummer with a booming voice and two dancers in traditional African dress paraded beside our table, chanting and yelling and singing at the top of their lungs. A belly dancer worked the other side of the restaurant. A fortuneteller sat at a table near the back, delivering good (or bad) news to the patrons. An artist in residence was painting near the center. The entire place pulsed with energy. It was unlike any restaurant experience we had ever had before. It was so good, in fact, that we both took our families back to it on other trips.

When was the last time you were not just impressed by a business, but wowed by it? It happens so rarely that when we experience it, it jolts us. We take notice. Remember the first time you saw an Apple Store? Have you ever been to a Disney theme park? What about the time you stayed at a hotel that was so amazing you didn't want to leave?

There are lots of very good businesses, but there are only a few that are truly something special. These organizations deliver great services or products, have top-notch customer relationships, and offer a special experience that is incomparable to others in their field. They may spawn competitors who try to duplicate their model, but rarely with the same success. These companies are simply remarkable.

It doesn't matter what profession we are talking about, nearly every business has the opportunity to be something remarkable. It could be a car dealership or a clothing store or concert venue. All of them have the chance to be extraordinary.

So if there can be awesome businesses in any field, when was the last time you saw a counseling or therapy practice that you would say was amazing? Not just a place with good therapists or nice offices, but something that was truly remarkable? Probably never.

And why not? Why couldn't there be a practice that blew you away, that far exceeded your expectations? Why couldn't there be a practice so remarkable that clients became fiercely loyal to it and other clinicians longed to be a part of it?

That's what this book is about. It's not about the mechanics of running a traditional private practice. It's about a framework for building a dream practice. It's about how to do something truly special. Something remarkable.

Our hope is to inspire you to new ways of thinking so you can build your own dream practice. In this book, we draw from our experiences in starting Southeast Psych in Charlotte, North Carolina. We hope to inspire you, challenge you, and stir you to action. We hope to push you beyond your fear to build something amazing—something that exceeds your wildest dreams.

Dave Verhaagen and Frank Gaskill
Charlotte, NC

I

The Essentials

one

Build the Foundation

A large ship was out in the middle of the ocean when the crew came running to the captain with terror in their eyes.

"Captain!" one of the men yelled, "There's a pirate ship on the horizon!"

"Bring me my red shirt!" the captain ordered. The men cut puzzled looks at each other but someone went down to the captain's quarters and brought him his red shirt, which he promptly put on and led the charge against the attackers, running off the pesky pirate ship.

A couple of days later, the crew ran to the captain again. This time, they looked even more terrified.

"Captain!" the same crewman yelled again, "This time there are *two* pirate ships!"

"Bring me my red shirt!" the captain commanded again.

And as before, the men brought the captain his red shirt, and after putting it on, he promptly beat back the pirate horde.

The crewmembers were all puzzled. That evening around dinner, one of the men asked the captain why he always called for his red shirt when the pirates came around.

"Because I'm the captain and it's my job to instill confidence in the crew," he explained. "So if I have to battle the pirates and I get cut or stabbed, I don't want people seeing me bleeding, so I call for the red shirt."

The crewmen all looked around at each other with nods of understanding.

A few days later, the crew came running to the captain, wide-eyed with fear.

"Captain," the man screamed, "Now there are *four* pirate ships!"

The captain set his jaw.

"Bring me my brown pants!" he said.

It's virtually guaranteed that if you start your own dream practice, you'll have more than a couple of brown-pants moments. We certainly did when we started Southeast Psych. We had never run a business before. In fact, we had never even taken a business class. So when we put both our houses on the line to take out a big bank loan to start an innovative private practice, you can be sure we both were wearing our brown pants on many days.

Now that Southeast Psych has grown into a large, thriving practice with several specialty brands, our own video studio and publishing arm, and a great reputation, it doesn't seem as risky. But when we started, it was pretty scary. Yet like most things in life, the greater the risk, the greater the potential reward. No matter how you slice it, starting your own dream practice is going to involve some risk. As you'll see, you manage that risk not by playing it safe but by being bold and equipping yourself to meet the challenges ahead. And the way you equip yourself is by thinking of yourself not only as a therapy practitioner but as a businessperson as well.

An Informal Business Education

A few years ago, Dave had lunch with a friend who was a successful businessman in town. They met in a nice restaurant and had an awesome, sprawling conversation about family, friends, and work. This friend loved his family, but he also really enjoyed his job. For him, work wasn't a chore; it was a privilege and a challenge. It delighted him. Dave asked him what he did for fun when he wasn't working.

"To be honest, I just like reading about business. I read business books and journals. I keep a stack of them on my bedside table."

"That's great," Dave said. But in his mind, he really didn't think it sounded that great. In fact, it sounded like a drag. He liked reading too, but the idea of reading a business journal on his downtime seemed about as appealing as having someone hit him in the face with a polo mallet. He did take away one key point, though: *Successful business people embrace business.* In graduate school, most helping professionals are given the message—implicitly or explicitly—that making a lot of money while helping people is unseemly. Sure, you can draw a salary and make a decent living, but much past that, you need to reexamine (and change) your motives.

Well, we would argue that to have a dream practice, you need to embrace business. And embracing business means you want to run a successful and profitable business. Running a successful business allows you to reinvest in your company and offer clients the services and experiences that fit their needs. This gives you the option of opening up greater access to some potential clients who may need discounted rates or pro bono services, all of which we have been able to do at Southeast Psych.

It's not enough to be a really good practitioner if you want to start and build your own dream practice. Many good clinicians have crashed and burned because they were unwilling or unable to embrace the fact that they were running a business. Years ago, we had an intern whom we were considering hiring full time after he finished his training. However, he decided to start his own one-man practice near downtown because he told us he was "philosophically opposed to marketing" and to other aspects of practice-building. You may not be surprised to hear that his practice was shuttered after a year, and he now works in a completely unrelated industry. He was a good clinician, but he wasn't willing or able to think of himself as a businessperson.

Early on, we quickly realized that to be successful in business, we had to think of ourselves as businesspeople. As obvious as this sounds, it's vital to your success. For this to work, you can't just be a clinician who happens to own a business; you must see yourself a businessperson who is starting a clinical practice. The difference there is essential.

Business is a discipline that has its own literature, its own best practices, and its own systems. Unfortunately for us, we had no business background. None at all. To say that we didn't have any business experience when we started the practice would be the understatement of the year. So some of our success was trial and error, but much of it was self-education. We read the best business books we could find. And we learned a ton from them. Here are just four examples of books that shaped our thinking and what we learned from each of them.

From *What Would Google Do?*, Jeff Jarvis (2009) exhorted us to decide what business we were in. This seems obvious, doesn't it? It's not. At the beginning, we were Southeast Psychological Services, but a few years into it, and after long conversations and a brainstorming retreat, we came to realize that we, Southeast Psychological Services, didn't just want to be in the psychological services business; we wanted to be in the *psychology business*. Our business was psychology, not just psychological services, like therapy and assessment and consultation. We were about psychology, and it could be in the form of traditional services, but also talks, videos, books, camps, and a bunch of other things we had yet to create. This prompted us to reshape our mission statement and even change our name to Southeast Psych. We only got there when we decided what business we were in.

From *Good to Great* by Jim Collins (2001), we learned three essential things: First, make sure you have the "right people on the bus." This means you hire the right people into the positions that fit them best. You want the right person to manage your office. You want the right person to take care of the finances. You want the right people to be your clinicians. You need the right people in the right spots. We'll talk more about this in our chapter on leading and managing. Second, Collins exhorts you to "find your hedgehog." This is the intersection of three overlapping circles: what you do best, what you feel most passionately about, and where you can make money. That sweet spot, that little "hedgehog," is what your business needs to be about. For us, it was psychology in the form of both services and products. Collins advises all of us to focus as much on what not to do as what to do. In other words, say no a lot. We did not heed that lesson well in the early days. We threw a lot of things at the wall to see what stuck, but over the years, as we have become more clear about what we are about, we have also said no to a lot of things that are great ideas but don't quite fit our mission. And although the book has many more key points, these three lessons helped us immensely in our earlier years.

From Michael Gerber's (1985) *E-Myth Revisited*, we learned that being a "technician"—a psychologist or a cake maker or a barber, and so on—who owns a business doesn't make you an entrepreneur. The notion that a technician is an entrepreneur just because he or she now owns the business is the "entrepreneurial myth," as Gerber coins it. Too many technicians fail because they continue working in their field and now have all the added responsibilities and frustrations of owning a business. Instead, Gerber preaches, you should work *on* your business, not *in* your business. A psychologist who stops working for an agency and decides to set up her own shop practicing psychology will have now have the business hassles that she hasn't been dealing with before on top of a full-time caseload of clients. Although for some this is a recipe for burnout, for others, it's more of a recipe for an inadequately developed business. We never fully got to Gerber's ideal (we both still practice psychology as part of our jobs), but we kept pushing ourselves closer to this model (carving out time for running the business, paying ourselves to run the business) the more we became aware of what it really takes to develop a business.

Finally, one of the most eye-opening, paradigm-shifting books for us was called *Blue Ocean Strategy*. We both use it as a reference throughout this book because it has influenced us so much. Authors W. Chan Kim and Renée Mauborgne (2005) note that most businesses in any given industry are in traditional territory that already has marked-out boundaries, expectations, and practices. However, in every field, there is the opportunity to be a Blue Ocean organization that pushes into uncharted territory. These are organizations that challenge the traditional boundaries of the profession. They do things that haven't been done before or stop doing things that were assumed to be essential to the industry. They do some things more than usual; they do other things less than usual. In other words, they remain within their industry but move into uncharted territory. So let's consider just five of the traditional expectations of a clinical practice are for a moment:

1. Quiet waiting area
2. Offices for therapy and testing
3. Appointments of a fixed length (50 minutes, etc.)
4. Check-in and checkout counter
5. Well-trained and licensed clinicians

Now which of these is essential? By our count, only one—the last one. There's no rule that says you have to have a traditional quiet waiting area, or a check-in/checkout area, or fixed-length appointments, or even traditional offices.

Thinking in Blue Ocean terms gets you thinking out of the traditional box. Ask yourself these four questions:

1. What are elements of traditional clinical practice we could do *more of?*
2. What are elements of traditional clinical practice we could do *less of?*
3. What are the elements of traditional clinical practice that we could do *stop doing?*
4. What are things that are not typically done in clinical practice that we could *start doing?*

Answering these questions gets you closer to Blue Ocean thinking. The authors make the point that Blue Ocean organizations represent a tiny proportion of any industry, but their research has found they tend to be more profitable than Red Ocean (e.g., more traditional) organizations. Yet profit alone isn't a good enough motive to become a Blue Ocean organization. The best motive for becoming a Blue Ocean is that you want to create an organization that lines up with your unique mission and values. For Southeast Psych, our mission is to "get psychology into the hands of as many people as possible to enhance their lives." It's a big, ambitious mission, but it has lit a fire under us. Our values are FIRE—Fun, Innovation, Relationship, and Excellence. Knowing and embracing our mission and values simplifies our decision-making grid. Now we run everything through the filter of these four questions:

1. Does it advance our mission?
2. Is it consistent with our values?
3. Do we have the resources for it?
4. Is it ethical?

So when we built a video studio, we didn't do it because we thought it was a cool idea (which it is) but because it furthered our mission of getting psychology out to as many people as possible in the form of short videos. And why do we want to do that? Because we believe psychology has the power to make people's lives better. When we put movie posters on the walls, gave every therapist a caricature by their door, and put full-sized superheroes in the hallways, it wasn't just because it was stuff we were interested in (which it is), but because it was fun and it makes psychology more accessible and appealing to people. And the more accessible and appealing it is, the more people it can help.

Our goal was to reshape the contours of the clinical service industry. And believe it or not, you can do the same thing, whether you are starting a group or even a solo practice.

Let's Dream Together

Let's see how this could look in real life. A therapist in Colorado named Karen wants to build her dream practice. She really has a passion for working with women and wants to build a practice around this specialty. She comes up with the name "Karen's Loft." The more she thinks about it, the more she likes it. It communicates exactly what she wants it to feel like: intimate, friendly, female-oriented, maybe a little bit of a secluded respite. Sometimes a name comes first, like it did for Karen, but often it flows from work on the mission statement. She'll stick with it for now, but she may have to come back later and make sure it lines up with her mission and values.

Karen takes an afternoon off to shape up her mission and values. After a few hours of writing and reflecting, she lands on a one-line mission statement: "Karen's Loft is a place for women to find support and experience personal growth through counseling and education." She likes it but doesn't love it. She can't tell if something's missing or if it's too limiting. Either way, she may need to double back and revise it. No problem for now.

The next step is to articulate her values. These values should be honest and authentic. They should embody what she really values. For Karen, these come to her easily. She values a feminist perspective, authentic relationships, a wholistic approach, and naturalistic strategies. She writes out the keywords:

- Feminist
- Authentic
- Wholistic
- Natural

She likes them. They capture what she's going for. She circles back to the mission statement. *Karen's Loft is a place for women to find support and experience personal growth through counseling and education.* Does she really want it to be "a place?" This sounds obvious, but maybe it's not. She decides that, yes, it needs to be a place. Okay, that works, but it definitely limits it to a physical location. It's not bad to limit yourself in a mission statement, but you need to make sure those are the limits you really want and need.

She moves on to the next phrase. Does she want it to focus on support and personal growth? Do those things get at what she wants to be about? Again, she decides yes. The final part of the statement is what seems to be a little off for her. She says she values a wholistic approach, but here she only mentions counseling and education. Is that too limiting? She'd love to have yoga on-site, support groups, and even a nutritionist. Why not? She decides she better cut that last phrase about counseling and education. Does she need to limit what services she offers in Karen's Loft? She may be personally limited in what she can do, but maybe she can find a way to offer services like yoga and nutrition support as an adjunct. She does, however, want to capture the wholistic nature of her practice. She lands on this final mission statement: *Karen's Loft is a place for women to find support and experience personal growth through care for the whole person.*

Then she begins imagining what this place needs to look like. She notices the values create the acronym FAWN and she's delighted by this little bit of serendipity. She wants to incorporate the deer theme into her logo. She likes the idea that the place might feel like a retreat center in the mountains. She begins to sketch out the feel of the place. It should have natural, unfinished timber for beams, she thinks. There should be pottery. There should be no TVs or other screens but lots of books in bookcases and on tables. They should serve green tea. There should be great folk music playing. The thoughts come to her in a rush. There should be cozy offices, yet at least one bigger space for groups and yoga. She can visualize the place in a way that fits perfectly with her mission and values. The physical place becomes an expression of the big ideas that made her want to do this in the first place. When it comes time to sink the extra money into the unplanned timber or the big meeting space, she won't hesitate because it has already become the logical conclusion of where she needs to go and what she needs to do.

We intentionally picked this example because it is so different from the look and feel of Southeast Psych. Karen wants a calm and peaceful vibe; we want a fun and energetic vibe. Karen wants a broader, wholistic experience that includes yoga; we focus only on psychology. The point of this book, then, is not to promote Southeast Psych as the model for psychological practice, but to say that your dream practice needs to flow from your dreams, from your unique calling and mission, and from your personal and professional values. The goal is for you to create your dream practice, not replicate ours. To do that, it's essential that you start with your own set of mission and values. You'll hear that refrain so many times in this book, it will make you shake your head and puff up your cheeks. But your eye-rolling isn't going to stop us! Everything we talk about is going to rest on the solid foundation of a clear mission statement and a well-articulated set of values. It's what lets you innovate, take risks, and dream big.

Be a Purple Cow

There was one other book that gave us a lot of encouragement. In *Purple Cow*, Seth Godin (2009) asks you to imagine what it would be like to see a herd of cows along the side of the road, all of them brown and nondescript, but in the middle of them all, there stands a single purple cow. Yes, a *purple cow*! Which cow do you notice? Which one stands out? The generic brown cows or the weird purple cow?

His point is obvious: If you want to have a remarkable business, you have to be different from the rest. You have to stand out from the herd. When we started Southeast Psych, we knew we wanted to create a purple cow, even though Godin's book hadn't come out yet. We knew we wanted to create something different and special.

In *Purple Cow*, Godin makes the claim that the opposite of remarkable is not bad, but *very good*. Don't miss this point. You could develop a practice that runs efficiently, has best practices for billing, and provides top-notch service, yet is just a really good brown cow. It's interchangeable from all the other good brown cows in your area.

To be a purple cow, you have to be remarkable; you have to stand out in some distinctive way; you have to take risks and not just stick to the safe, tried-and-true meadows that are the territory of the brown cowherd. Godin suggests you find things that are just not done in your line of work and go ahead and do them anyway. For Southeast Psych, we recently offered a "Super Conference" to the community featuring 20 experts talking about their specialties—their best stuff—in hour-long breakout sessions. It was packed! Nearly every workshop was full of parents, educators, and other professionals. That's not too distinctive, you're probably thinking. And you'd be right, except that we didn't charge a nickel for it. It was completely free. Twenty hours of continuing education from some of the best professionals anywhere with hundreds of attendees, and we didn't ask for a dime. Does that sound a little crazy? Here's crazier: One year we also leased a booth at the American Psychological Association national convention just so we could invite people to play video games with us. We had nothing to sell but fun. We wanted people to catch a vision of how the practice of psychology could look different. It cost us a small fortune, but the consensus was that we would do it again in a heartbeat, so for several years after that, we set up our studios in a double-booth at the national conventions in Boston, San Francisco, Orlando, and Washington, DC to film interviews, run game shows, and just have fun. Even the conference organizers had no idea what to make of us. We are forever doing things that are fun and unusual.

So, in addition to starting with "Why?" you follow up with Seth Godin's "Why not?" to stress test your ideas a little. Why have a video studio? Because it furthers our mission of getting psychology into the hands of as many people as possible to enhance their lives. Why not? Besides pragmatic concerns (time and resources), there's really no reason a psychology practice can't do that. The fact that others aren't doing it is irrelevant. Being a purple cow means asking "why not?" a lot.

A word of caution: If you intend to be a purple cow, some people will not like you. And those people will typically be others in your profession. When we first started producing videos, many of them were just meant to be silly and funny. One had a clip of a therapy session reenacted as a Spanish soap opera; another showed one of us riding down the street on a kid's three-wheeled bike called a Green Machine; still another showed our "Festivus" celebration (a *Seinfeld* reference) that included "feats of strength" in which guests tried to wrestle the host to the ground. One day, we received a forwarded e-mail that was a discussion thread from a couple of out-of-town psychologists who had seen these silly videos online. We have long since deleted the e-mail, but it went something like this:

Brown Cow 1: I watched those videos. Do you think it's unethical to put something like that out there?

Brown Cow 2: I don't think it's unethical. It may be kind of unprofessional. It's not something I would do.

Brown Cow 1: Neither would I. I just don't know what they are trying to accomplish.

Brown Cow 2: Yeah, it's definitely weird.

Brown Cow 1: They're just immature fools.

That last quote is verbatim. After this, we started calling ourselves "immature fools," which gained a lot of comedy traction around our place for a while. You get the point, though, that these professionals were upset because this was something that just wasn't done. It was unusual. Out of the norm. Unsettling.

Exactly!

We created the videos to signal that we were about fun, something that psychology practices are not known for, to say the least. We posted the videos to be disruptive. Not to be hurtful and certainly not to be unethical, but to send a message that we were doing things differently. We became aware of lots of furrowed brows and hand wringing among other psychologists, but not from clients. They loved the videos and wanted more of them. But be aware that if you want to be different, some people—maybe even many people—won't like you.

A large newspaper ran a flattering story about us but also quoted another psychologist that I don't believe either of us have ever met saying that Southeast Psych "trivializes much of what is important" in the practice of psychology. He didn't elaborate on what those important things were or how we trivialized them, but it was clear he was none too happy with how we did things. To be honest, we were glad for the quote because it made for a better story—all good stories have conflict and opposition—and it let readers decide for themselves if that seemed to be true. If some people read the story and concluded they never wanted to set foot in our place, then we would be grateful they screened themselves out. However, it also exposed us to thousands of potential new clients, some of whom called to schedule first-time appointments because of what they had read.

As long as you aren't doing something unethical or truly unprofessional, then don't worry about opposition. If you are doing something innovative or new or different, you will have your naysayers and your haters. Nearly any cool thing worth doing is going to be met with resistance, especially from others in the field. And if you are successful, your opposition will likely increase. Brown cows don't like purple cows. It's a fact of nature.

We love the study psychologists Justin Hepler and Dolores Albarracin (in press) did in which they asked a group of 200 men and women how they felt about a bunch of fairly random things like crossword puzzles, camping, the country of Japan, taxidermy, recycling, and so on. They noted the raters who tended to judge harshly. We'll call them "the haters." The haters tended to dislike most things, having unfavorable opinions about many unrelated subjects. A month later, they asked everyone to do the ratings again to make sure they weren't just in an especially grumpy mood that day. When they established the group of reliable haters, they gave them information about a new product, a microwave oven (the "Monahan LPI-800 Compact 2/3-Cubic-Foot 700-Watt Microwave Oven," to be exact). They were also given three awesome reviews about the new product, gushing over how great it was, as well as three negative reviews that expressed dissatisfaction with the new microwave oven. Oh, by the way, there was also no such thing as the Monahan LPI-800. It was a fake product, and the reviews were also completely made up. What they found probably won't surprise you. People who tended to like crossword puzzles and Japan and taxidermy (and other random things) also said they liked what they learned about the new microwave oven. The haters, by contrast, hated the fake new oven. Hepler and Albarracin write, "Someone's attitude toward architecture may, in fact, tell us something about their attitude toward health care because both attitudes would be biased by a disposition to like or dislike stimuli."

Simply put, haters are gonna hate. If you're going to be a purple cow, it's going to happen. Don't worry about it.

Start With Why

In one of the most viewed TED Talks of all time, Simon Sinek states, "People don't buy what you do; people buy *why* you do it." He gives the example of Apple, a company that has revolutionized modern life in some unexpected ways and with some unexpected products. Whereas other companies start with what they do, Apple starts with why it does it. To paraphrase, Apple would say, "With everything we do, *we believe in challenging the status quo.* The way we challenge the status quo is by making our products beautifully designed, simple to use, and user-friendly. We just happen to make good computers and phones and tablets. Would you like to buy one?"

Other companies start with the *what* (we make great widgets), then go to the *how*, and then sometimes get to the *why*. Apple starts with the *why* (we believe in challenging the status quo, in thinking differently), then they go to the how, then they get to the *what*.

At Southeast Psych, we start with the *why* (we believe psychology can enhance people's lives), then go to the *how* (by getting it to as many people as possible), then to the *what* (through psychological services and products). Before you begin your dream practice, start with your *why*. Why are you doing this? It's not just to make a living. That's a natural result of a good business, not the reason for doing it. It's not just to provide clinical services (that's the what). Clearly answer the question of *why* you do what you do, then let the rest work itself out naturally.

Everything we talk about in this book makes the most sense when you know why you are doing these things. When you know why, it lets you say yes to the right things and no to the misaligned things. When you know why, it shapes your decisions and makes your business something special. It truly lets you build your dream practice.

In the chapters to come, you'll read a lot about things like creating a culture, connecting with your community, and having the right mindset for the success of your dream practice. What you won't get is much of the minutia of running a practice. We won't talk about billing, record keeping, scheduling software, reviewing lease agreements, and the million other details you might need to know to run a successful practice. Those are important things, but that's another book. This book is about the big stuff and the deeper stuff. It's not just about being a practitioner who owns a business. It's about creating your dream practice.

You better put on your brown pants.

two

Create a Culture

Two young fish were happily swimming along through a coral reef, laughing and chasing each other, when they came across an older fish going in the other direction.

"Afternoon, boys. How's the water?" the older fish asked them as they passed by.

The two younger fish swam off with puzzled looks on their faces. Finally, one of the fish looked over at the other and asked, "What the hell is water?"

Often the most obvious and most important realities of our lives are the ones that are the hardest to see. Fish aren't aware of water; humans aren't aware of oxygen. And in organizations, we aren't much better at noticing organizational culture. Every organization—a family, a club, a business—has a culture. That culture has been created either intentionally or unintentionally, but it's there nonetheless. We may not even be fully aware of the culture on a day-to-day, moment-to-moment basis, even though it is the essence of that organization. In fact, all the values of that organization are embedded and lived out in that culture.

Whether you are in a solo or group practice, you have the opportunity to create a culture. If you are starting from scratch, you have the chance to start fresh and build the kind of culture you want. However, if you are part of an existing practice that already has some of its invisible culture in place, you can still re-create that culture. In fact, you must re-create it. It's essential to having your dream practice.

Unintentional Organizational Culture

Dave became aware of organizational culture early in his career during his internship. He had a terrific time that year, which was spent on a large residential campus for severely mentally ill teenagers. The kids, though struggling with severe mental illness, were great fun. They were spontaneous and loose, and would say and do things that were often delightful. They put on musicals and had an awesome prom. The style of these kids infected the tone of the entire campus. Even the staff was a blast. Influenced by the great Pam Abraham, now a professor at Immaculata College, the staff team was funny and playful and quite different from other psychologists and residential staff he had known before. Without realizing it at the time, their sense of playfulness probably laid the foundation for Southeast Psych's culture of fun—or at least gave tacit permission to try it.

The next year for his postdoctoral fellowship, Dave worked for a community organization that served highly aggressive kids in a continuum of care, ranging from outpatient therapy to locked residential facilities. These kids were the real deal. In fact, to be served by the program, you had to have committed multiple acts of serious violence. One teenage client had beaten a man to death; another had committed a carjacking, holding a gun on a woman and her young children. The tone of that staff team was serious, straightforward, no-nonsense, and assertive. It was easy to understand why. The client population seemed to demand it.

These two organizations had very different cultures that had formed around the populations they served. It was a great study in contrasts. The internship helped sweet kids who were loosely connected in their thinking; the postdoc helped angry kids who pushed boundaries. Consequently, the cultures had wrapped around these populations and the tone and themes and ways of relating became dictated by the groups they served. This isn't an entirely bad thing, but what became clear was these two organizations had unintentionally allowed their cultures to be shaped, rather than purposefully creating the waters in which they swam. Despite having great clinicians in both groups, we doubt there was a single person in either who could articulate the themes of their organizational culture. For them, it was invisible. It was just a how things were, the way things had to be.

Organizational culture can be shaped by who you serve, but it can also be molded unintentionally by the personalities of those who lead them, for either good or bad. A few years later, Dave joined a group practice, and the leader of that group was a highly anxious person. When managed care threatened to dominate our industry, you could feel the anxiety grip him—and, consequently, the entire group. Much time was spent on developing policies and flowcharts and other ways to "survive" the onslaught of managed care. The tone of the practice was dictated by the leader's own anxiety.

There's no question your practice's culture will be, in some way, shaped by your personality and the other dominant personalities in the organization. But there is a difference between allowing this to unintentionally shape your culture versus being intentional with your culture creation. The fact that a life-size Darth Vader stands near our entrance and a full-size Storm Trooper guards the checkout is a testament to Frank's influence and personality. It's not a coincidence that we have a *Star Wars* theme throughout the place. The fact that there are movie posters and superhero caricatures down the hallways is a reflection of what both of us enjoy.

But we would argue that we didn't just casually fall into having these themes and visuals; they were in line with our values of fun and innovation. And when we did our space planning, we intentionally placed our video studio in the front behind a solid wall of glass where people could see it rather than in the back where it wouldn't be as conspicuous. Why? Because we wanted people to ask "Why?" Because we wanted it to be eye-catching and pique the curiosity of our clients, visitors, and the hundreds of people who worked on the other 10 floors of our building and walked by it every day on their way in and out of the office building. Because we wanted to signal to our staff that we were serious about our mission of pushing psychology outside of these walls. In other words, it was done intentionally.

Intentional Organizational Culture

You intentionally create a culture by first becoming clear about your mission and values. Without those, you have no anchor, and your culture develops only around personalities of your leaders or the traits of your client population or other demands of the job. Once you have a clearly described mission and set of values, you can then go about the business of shaping the culture you want. For us to get psychology into the hands of as many people as possible to enhance their lives, we have to push psychology out of our physical space to expand our reach. This gives an almost "missionary vibe" to our culture. Our values are fun, innovation, relationship, and excellence, so this informs how we do meetings, how we budget, how we connect with each other, how we hire. The most common bit of feedback we get from visitors and new clients is, "This place is so fun!" That's not by accident. It's because we value fun and we intentionally infuse our culture with it.

So how do we make it fun? Here are some of the components.

- **We hire fun people.** We're looking for fun people when we interview, people with senses of humor, people who do fun things, people who have fun personalities. Not everyone is the life of the party or a comedian, but everyone has a sense of fun.
- **We openly discuss our value of fun.** We bring it up in staff meetings and trainings, we include it in written communications, and we tell others about it. In other words, we keep the value of fun fresh in our minds by reminding each other of it.
- **We create opportunities for fun.** We watch movies together and play games, we insert fun elements into meetings, we create dumb contests ("March Family Madness," where we try to top each other with crazy family stories or awkward family photos, for example), we have nonsense on the walls of our lounge ("Best pranks of the year," "Evidence that Dave is actually a zombie," etc.), and a bunch of other things signaling that this is a place where fun happens.
- **We socialize together.** We have events where staff and their families can get together and do something fun (a corn maze, a barbecue, movie nights, theme parties, 5K races, etc.). The

better people know each other outside of work, the more fun they have together.

- **We evaluate our fun progress.** One of the questions we often ask in leadership meetings is, "How much fun did we have this year?" or "What have we been doing lately that has been fun?" If we are serious about the value of fun, we need to make sure we're intentional about it. Paradoxically, the more we are intentional about it, the more spontaneously it happens. It has just become part of the fabric of our organization.

Again, we're not advocating that your practice needs to value fun, per se. It's certainly a good fit for us, but it is definitely not the right gig for everyone. What we are advocating, however, is that you are clear about what you do value and then become intentional about how to make that a part of your culture. As such, your values should give shape and contour to the practice culture. Imagine what a culture might look like if it was shaped around one or more of these values:

- Risk taking
- Justice
- Spirituality
- Community service
- Authenticity
- Change
- Strength focused

All of these are good values, but you can see how adopting a particular one of these (or any number of dozens of other values) might inform and shape your culture. As good as these and other values are, it's vital to carefully select your core values to reflect what you want your practice to be about. Dave personally values healthy risk taking, but it's not one of our organizational values. It doesn't mean we don't take risks, but it does mean that it isn't necessarily a daily, lived out value of the organization. Dave values justice, but, again, it isn't a core part of what we are doing with our practice. It doesn't mean it isn't important; it just means that it is not what we exist to be about on a daily basis. Perhaps it will be for your practice. If so, own it and shape your organizational culture around it.

The Physical Aspects of Culture

We've been in dozens of psychological and psychiatric practices, and most of them are, to use Seth Godin's term, "brown cows." The waiting rooms are typically drab with furniture that feels like it came from a yard sale or a used office furniture store, old pictures that are slightly less depressing than TAT cards, and linoleum floors or well-worn carpet. We visited one practice a few years ago that had a few issues of *Newsweek* magazine that were two years old, which would have made for good reading if you wanted to know the big news stories of the previous midterm election cycle.

The message of these waiting areas—and there is a message here—is that these spaces are unimportant. They are holding tanks for you to sit until your service is provided. Even practices that try a little harder by adding some relaxing music or a little water sculpture on a side table miss a huge opportunity. The waiting area experience communicates volumes to your clients.

This was one of our first big realizations. The physical space helps shape culture, and vice versa. After you check in, just past the video studio, you come around the corner to see a small bookstore with a stylish couch and chairs facing a big screen TV. Just beyond that, our hostess sits at a stand and offers you coffee, tea, or lemonade; if you are in the mood, she will engage you in conversation, but if not, she simply greets you warmly. Behind her is a small kid's room with two flat screen TVs, one for movies and TV shows and the other for video games. Around the corner is another, larger waiting area with sofas and small round tables with comfortable chairs. On the walls are bright works of art by local artists, much of it available for sale. The whole vibe is positive, interesting, and even fun.

A nice waiting area communicates care for the client; a bland waiting room area communicates doing things on the cheap. The same goes for the rest of the place. If you have a practice where a receptionist sits behind glass, for example, you may be signaling things like "distance," "old school," "medical model." If you want to telegraph these things, then go for it, but if not, then think about what every part of your space says to the client. Specifically, think about these areas:

- Front door
- Check-in
- Waiting area
- Hallways
- Your therapy office
- Testing rooms
- Rest rooms
- Other public spaces

You may not have all of these areas in your space, but consider what you do have and what message it sends to the client. The physical space is a vital part of the culture you intend to create. Ask yourself, "If I was seeing this for the first time, what assumptions would I have about this place, these therapists, and the services they deliver?"

The Emotional Aspects of Culture

Coming into a business is not just about goods and services; it's also about an experience. Dave and his wife recently went out to dinner at a newly opened restaurant not far from their house. The place was open and light. There was a gelato bar ablaze with color. They were greeted warmly, the service was excellent, the manager came by to check on them, and the food was good. As they left, the owner and manager thanked them for coming. Would they go back? Of course. Not because the food was the best in town, but because the whole experience from the first greeting to the final thank you and everything in between was special.

In an individual or group practice, you want people to have the same experience. Yes, you want to be the best therapist in town, but you also want the whole package to be entirely extraordinary. You have three audiences you are serving with this experience: clients, staff (both clinical and support), and other visitors. So you ask yourself:

What do I want it to feel like to be a client here?

What do I want it to feel like to work here?

What do I want it to feel like to visit here?

To use Southeast Psych as an example again, we want clients to have *fun*, to feel *optimistic*, and to feel *respected*. So our place is designed to accomplish this, including not only how the place looks and feels, but also how the staff interacts, how we do staff training, and how the client is cared for at every phase. We look at the experience as a whole organism. The greeting, the waiting, the clinical service, the checkout, and all the little parts in between are part of a full experience.

We want our staff to feel respected, heard, and valued. We want the experience of work to be that this is the best possible place they could be. We don't believe in no-compete clauses because we believe not having them keeps the burden on us to create the best work environment possible. There are people who work for us that know they could make more money if they struck out on their own, but they couldn't have a better work experience, a better group of work friends, or a better network of professional support.

For us, it's also important to dump the hierarchy. You can't tell from the website or the letterhead or the size of the offices who is a partner or who is on the leadership team. Similarly, you can't tell from a lunch meeting or a social event who is on the clinical staff and who is a part of the support staff. Everyone is treated with the same regard and respect.

We know of a health care company that makes everyone wear their ID badges in a visible location with their degree in giant letters and their name in small letters. The message is apparent the minute you walk in: An MD is higher on the food chain, then a PhD, then an MA, and so on. That little nametag sends a big message. There is definitely a pecking order in that organization, and they are parading it around like roosters.

During Dave's internship year, he got the chance to supervise an undergraduate student who was in the process of applying to graduate schools. He got an interview at a school, and when he got there, he realized it was a group interview where all the applicants were placed in a room and instructed to have a conversation about who among them should be admitted and who should be rejected. After he relayed this story, Dave told him that if this was the only program that admitted him, he'd be wise not to go; the school was sending an early message about how he would be treated there. People are incredibly nervous about these interviews to start with, and then to subject them to such an experience says that they were more interested in their little experiment than caring for the applicants. (A postscript to this story is that this was in fact the only program that admitted him that year; he heeded the advice and sat out a year before reapplying for a position.)

These examples of a nametag or a group interview seem small, but they tell us a lot about how people are treated, subtly or not so subtly, by the organization. What does it feel like to work there (or study there, or even visit there)? The point is that every organization sends a message to everyone it interacts with at nearly every point of contact, from its brochures to its online presence to its staff meetings to pretty much everything else.

We even want each visitor, including those interviewing with us, individuals representing other organizations, or media professionals, as three examples, to have a great experience. We want them to go back and tell other people that this was something special. It doesn't matter if they represent a network of residential programs or a printing company or an online marketing firm, we want all our guests to feel like they are treated with respect and had a little bit of fun. A great example of this was when a reporter for a large paper came by to do a story about the two of us speaking at a national convention. It was supposed to be a little story, but when the reporter came to our place, she was so wowed by the experience, she re-envisioned the whole piece and made it a story about how our practice was a new model for psychological practice. You'll hear more about that story in our final chapter.

Creating an organizational culture has much to do with how you treat people, but it also has to do with your expectations of them as well. In our place, it is not okay for a clinician to disrespect a member of the support staff—ever! It's also expected that each person will build relationships with others in the practice. It's expected that conflict will be addressed directly. It's part of having a culture that values healthy, open relationships. The expectation is there, and each person is held to it. Like any human system, we fail at this at times, but we are always striving to uphold the ideal.

Believe it or not, we also have expectations for the behavior of our clients or potential clients. When they work with us, we respect them and they respect us. That means all of us, including our support staff. Here is an example. A mother of a teenager called to make an appointment for her son whom she recently discovered had relapsed with his drug problem. She was frazzled and at her wit's end, which is completely understandable, but when she called, she was so demanding and rude that it left our staff member, who was trying to help her, in tears. This staff person relayed this story to Dave, and he called the mother directly and told her that we wouldn't be able to work with her because we didn't allow our staff to be treated disrespectfully. The woman cried and apologized and explained how stressful this had all been for her. She said she would be willing to call the staff member back and apologize directly. Dave told her that if she would be willing to do this, then he would gladly change his mind about seeing her son. She closed the conversation by saying, "I appreciate what you're doing. I work for someone myself, and I wish they would stick up for me the way you are sticking up for your employees." Dave ended up seeing the young man, who made a ton of progress. Dave was so grateful she was able to hear him out and respond so well. Had she not, he would not have agreed to work with them because it's important for us to send the message that we have expectations that all of us—clients included— respect everyone in our shop. We would rather lose 20 clients who were entitled and disrespectful than keep them all and have them treat our staff poorly. The notion that the customer is always right is quite simply wrong. They're not. No one person or group of people is always right. For us, this business is not just about an exchange of money for a service, it's about a mutually respectful relationship.

Constant Attention to Culture

A few years ago, we would have said you have to intentionally create a culture, but once it is set, the organization perpetuates that culture, as long as the people in the organization buy into the mission and values.

Boy, were we wrong.

We like being cultural architects, but what we've come to realize is it isn't enough to create it; you have to manage it. Without nearly constant nurturance and attention, the culture begins to slip off the rails. At first, it is ever-so-slightly, almost imperceptibly, but then it happens in major ways that take some heavy lifting to get it back on track.

Several years ago, we hit one of our growth spurts, and we decided it was finally time to open a second office. But we only wanted to do it if it had the DNA of Southeast Psych and wasn't just another group practice office in town. It needed to share our mission and values; it needed to have our culture of fun and playfulness and innovation.

After a lot of deliberation, we found the perfect location in a growing area in the southern part of the city in the Blakeney area, a little more than 20 minutes away from our main office. We would create space for about eight full-time therapists. We had daylong planning retreats, some of them specifically dedicated to the issue of encoding our culture in the new location. About half of the staff would be transplants, but the other half would be new to us. They had never worked at Southeast Psych before. It was essential for them to get what we were really about. They had to understand the mission and values and show commitment to them. Frank and I decided to stay with the mothership, but we sent out some capable staff and leaders to help pioneer the new venture.

We designed the space intentionally, giving it a coffee-shop feel. It was even more gorgeous than the main office. We made sure each therapist had his or her superhero caricature and that the hallway had giant superhero decals on the wall. We talked to the staff about our distinctives—a sense of fun and playfulness, innovation and creativity, direct and authentic relationships. Everyone seemed to be on board.

A few years into it, we all agreed the Blakeney office was hugely successful in terms of revenue, productivity, and client and staff satisfaction. In fact, the per-therapist revenue was better than at our bigger office. Every single therapist also said they loved working there. But we also agreed that it was functioning like just another good group practice office. It didn't have the Southeast Psych DNA—or if it did, it wasn't being expressed. There was not the same sense of fun and spontaneity. Relationships were pleasant and cooperative, but most everyone seemed to be running their own solo practices. While the main office was experiencing an explosion of innovation in many ways, the Blakeney office seemed to be getting increasingly more traditional. Again, there was nothing bad about it. From a revenue standpoint, it was actually going gangbusters. But from a culture standpoint, it was far from Southeast Psych.

When a staff issue needed to be resolved, Dave had some meetings with a few of the Blakeney therapists who sheepishly gave their opinions of what they thought needed to happen but seemed fearful of speaking their mind. To be honest, it shocked him. At the main office, we were used to staff speaking their minds on an almost daily basis. One of the Blakeney therapists even gave her input, then hastened to add, "But I don't want to lose my job," clearly communicating she didn't think it was safe to speak honestly. Dave thought our high staff retention and job satisfaction spoke for itself. We weren't blowing people out of there for speaking their minds. At that point, we knew something was really wrong. We had worked hard to create a culture of openness, honesty, mutual respect, but here was someone—and a few others like her—who was scared of losing her job for expressing an opinion.

When we thought about the staff team and leadership at Blakeney, there wasn't a soul there who wasn't kind and supportive and respectful. We realized the person who had said this had never worked with us in the main office and, in fact, had previously worked for a big health care organization that had an entirely different culture than ours. In that organization, we could imagine it would not be looked upon with favor to express a dissenting opinion. In ours, it's what we wanted. But somehow she didn't know that and certainly didn't feel that.

After a lot of conversations with the leadership team and a lot of deliberation, we realized the issues with Blakeney—our failure to translate our culture to the new office—didn't come down to one of our leaders doing something wrong. It came down to our lack of attention to it. As the primary cultural architect, Dave thought it was enough to wind it up and it would run well on its own once we got the right people on the bus and the right messages to them. But it wasn't. We weren't out there, so we didn't have our ears to the ground well enough to sense what was happening on a day-to-day, week-to-week basis. By the time we were fully tuned into it, it was off the rails.

It's not enough to create a culture; you have to deliberately manage a culture. And because the Blakeney office was successful from a financial and business standpoint, we assumed it was going fine culturally. Again, to make it clear we are not saying the main office was so awesome and the Blakeney office wasn't. Not at all. Depending on what metric you used, the Blakeney office might come out on top. What we are saying, though, is that while Blakeney was a successful group practice office, it lacked the emotional buy-in to our values of fun, innovation, and relationships (though it was high on excellence) and it didn't have the culture that flowed out of those values. The latter—the buy-in to mission and values—trumps the business success, at least for us. We would rather not make as much revenue with an office fully invested in our mission and values than have them make a ton more money and not have that same commitment.

Over the past couple of years, we've worked hard to address the cultural issues at Blakeney. We have a leadership team made up of clinicians from both offices, all of them fully committed to living out our mission in a working culture that is informed and shaped by our values. But it's hard work and it requires our constant attention.

Whether you are in a solo or group practice, you have the opportunity to create a culture that expresses your true values. But creating it is not enough. You have to manage it. And that takes a lot of work and complete dedication. It will be worth it, though, because a vibrant, intentional culture is at the very heart of creating your dream practice.

three

Think Abundance

In order to succeed, your desire for success must
be stronger than your fear of failure.
—*Bill Cosby*

Years ago, we were recruiting a neuropsychologist for our practice. Dave had a phone interview with this really sharp guy. He was heavily courted, coming right out of a top-ranked doctoral program.

"So who in town will I be taking business from?" he asked toward the end of the interview.

"What do you mean?" Dave was genuinely confused by the question.

"Well, if I come into town and I do well, who will I be taking business away from?" he clarified.

"I really don't know," Dave said. "We don't really think like that."

"Well," he said. "It's just logical. If I'm doing well, then that means someone else is losing business."

To his credit, it was one of the first times we had heard a psychologist talking in business terms right out of graduate school, so we had to hand it to him in that regard. But we also knew almost immediately after that comment that he was not going to be a good fit for us.

Why? Because he was thinking in scarcity terms. His thinking, which is prevalent in many businesses, is that there are a limited number of resources to go around and you must scrap for what you get, essentially taking away business from your competitors. Now this may be true in some businesses, like selling cell phones or luxury cars, but it's not true in health care. In mental health care, the research says only about 40% of the people who actually need our services actually seek and receive our services (McLean, 2012). What this means is that there is far more unmet need than we realize.

So back to our recent grad hotshot. When Dave told him he wouldn't be taking business away from anyone if he did well, he challenged him on it.

"I don't understand how that can be. Can you explain your thinking on that?"

"Well, there are more people who need our services than receive them in this community. The trick is for us to create greater awareness and access, then provide a superior product, and not to start throwing elbows with competitors for market share."

He wasn't convinced and he told us so. We pleasantly ended the conversation but we both knew it wasn't going to work out. Our philosophies of practice development were too incompatible. (His job ultimately went to Craig Pohlman, who has since become our CEO.) We use this young professional as an example not to ridicule his position. In fact, it's a perfectly reasonable stance, and one that many businesses take. We bring up this conversation to draw an important contrast. He was thinking in terms of scarcity; we think in terms of abundance.

Scarcity thinkers tend to see a finite pie with limited slices. They fight for a bigger slice and wring our hands over how much of the pie the other guy has. It makes good sense, of course. There can't be an infinite pie with unlimited slices, can there?

No, but the pie might be much bigger than you imagined. And maybe, to go back to our Blue Ocean thinking, we might even decide to bake a new pie. That's how abundance thinkers think.

Let us pause and say that we are not some prosperity gurus promising you great riches or selling unlimited success. We're simply advocating a different way of thinking. Scarcity thinking is the product of fear and leads to paralysis and making only safe, "brown cow" choices. It breeds unhealthy competitiveness and jealousy. It can also make you self-centered and tight-fisted.

By contrast, abundance thinking is all about the notion that there is a world of opportunity out there. We need to dream big, put ourselves out there boldly, and deliver excellent service and products. In doing so, we take risks, make innovative choices, and feel the freedom to support and even nurture our competitors. It's a very different way of thinking, and it leads to very different outcomes.

Abundance Thinking Promotes Generosity

A large health care organization in town decided to close their child and adolescent mental health services unit, leaving several really good therapists stranded without jobs. We met with a few of them to talk about the possibility of opening up another office for them. It sounded like a win–win: They would have jobs, and we would have more presence in the downtown area. But as we talked and debated this through with our leadership team, we decided it was not the time for us to open another office. We were already running on all cylinders with our two locations, and we felt like a third office would have just overtaxed us and our staff. We decided to pass on the idea, but we also wanted to help these folks out. We posed the idea of them starting their own practice in the downtown area with our support. We would consult with them, encourage them, and open up our business practices to them. They took us up on the offer and now have a solid practice in that vital part of the city. We feel good about referring to them and vice versa. When they opened up this new practice, we didn't suffer, even when they added staff. In fact, we only benefitted by the increase in goodwill and professional relationships.

In *Give and Take*, Adam Grant (2014) argues that professionals tend to have one of three different styles: *takers, matchers,* and *givers.* Takers try to get as much as they can from others. The message they send in their professional activities is: "I'm here to get something from you, not to give something to you." Matchers want to have equivalent "quid pro" interactions with others. Relationships with matchers are purely transactional, functioning almost like contracts. They give to others, but they want to get in return. Givers are the rare people who desire to contribute to others with no expectation that they will benefit from doing so. Grant argues persuasively with compelling research that givers frequently achieve an astonishingly high degree of excellent success and results across a wide range of industries. Even though some givers get burned out and mistreated, most seem to thrive. They not only do well themselves, but they help others along the way and have a depth of character that most others can't match.

Scarcity thinking makes it hard to be anything other than a taker or matcher. Abundance thinking frees you up to be a giver.

Locus of Control Applied

We've consulted with professionals working in major metropolitan areas that are known for having market saturation. In these areas, it is widely believed there is a glut of providers; too many people are competing for too few resources. Despite this, many of these up-and-coming professionals have been able to build highly successful practices. Scarcity thinking would say, "There's too much competition." Abundance thinking says, "There's always room for something exceptional."

It's what you learned in your training about locus of control. Students who believe their good effort is likely to result in good grades are more likely to be academically successful than those who believe their future rests on outside factors like good (or bad) luck or whether the teacher favored them or not. For those who want to create a dream practice, those who believe they can make a good living in a competitive marketplace are much more likely to do well than those who don't have this belief. This isn't mystical nonsense; it's what we know about how humans achieve and succeed.

The abundance mindset is not just a peripheral point. In our view, it merits a full chapter and a fair discussion because without it, it is unlikely you will succeed. In fact, it is one of the top three factors that predict success. What are those three factors? Simple, first, you must be good at what you do. Second, you must be willing to connect relationally in your community. Third, you must have an abundance mindset.

Why is this mindset so important? Because it undergirds the whole effort. Let us contrast abundance thinking with its opposite, scarcity thinking. Let's use the example of Jay, a psychologist who had been working for a community mental health agency in a sunny southern state. He's a good therapist and probably one of the best diagnosticians in his area. He had set a five-year timeline for working in an agency, and that time was now about done. He felt genuinely good about his time in community mental health. It was challenging, for sure, but it was also rewarding to be able to serve people who often didn't have access to good help. But now he had the experience under his belt, a three-year-old toddler at home, and another baby on the way. He was ready to be on his own, but he was more than a little freaked out by it. He consulted with a financial planner who told him he'd need at least a $50,000 loan just to open his one-man operation. He was still paying back student loans, and he and his wife had a mortgage and two car payments. Fifty grand sounded like too much to him. *What if it doesn't work? What if I don't get referrals?*

He looked at a directory of local therapists and flipped through it page after page. There were so many of them—and many who were doing exactly what he wanted to do, seeing the same clients he wanted to see. It was discouraging. *Honestly, how much business can there be in town?* he thought to himself. *Surely all these people can't be successful.*

He decided to do a smart thing. He set up lunch appointments with a few of his would-be competitors to gather some intel. He discovered what he already suspected to be true: Many of them were taking big cuts to be on managed care panels. Others only had part-time practices. A few had nested themselves in medical practices to be at the beck and call of the physicians. A few, however, seemed to be doing just fine. He couldn't figure out what separated the successful ones from the others. They all seemed to be nice people. They all seemed to have a pretty good sense of what they were doing. Maybe it was the luck of the draw? Maybe it was just people who had been in town longer? Either way, it seemed only to reinforce his idea that the venture he was considering was incredibly risky.

Feeling overly cautious, he decided to join a collective in town and rent some office space. He contracted for three days a week for only $500 a month. It seemed like a great deal. It was safe and the chances of it sinking him financially were low. It was far from the $50,000 loan and all the risks associated with it. So for three years, he saw about 20 to 24 clients a week for assessment and therapy. His overhead costs were low, and his profit margin was fairly high. He had a decent stream of referrals, and there were some professionals in town who thought he was great and routinely sent clients his way.

So why was he so unhappy? At first he thought it was the usual anxieties of private practice, the wildly unpredictable paychecks, and the worries about referrals. Then he thought it was because he was kind of lonely. This was a group only in name; all the therapists did their own thing and just shared space, seeing each other occasionally in the hallway. Finally, though, he realized he was feeling a loss of something bigger. This practice of his was just like everyone else's, and he had long had a dream of doing something special (being a purple cow). But doing the special thing was incredibly risky—50K risky, to be exact!

One Friday morning, he went to a coffee shop and left his laptop at home. Instead, he had a journal and pen and spent a couple of hours writing. Some of it was longhand, but some of it was just bullet points or phrases. He drew boxes and circles around some of what he wrote and connected other points with lines and arrows. By the end of the time, though, it was all clear to him. He wrote a summary sentence: "I've been so worried about failure that I have not taken any chances and because of that, I have denied myself the opportunity to create something really cool and special."

That's what this book is about at its heart. It's about creating something special. It's not about the mechanics of running a practice—the business planning and bookkeeping and billing. No, it's about creating the special thing, the thing that is unique to you. And there's no way around it, except to acknowledge that you have to push through fear and take a risk. Whether that risk is a large loan or enlisting others to join you in an untested venture or some other equally scary thing, there is still risk involved. And if you begin, like Jay, with scarcity thinking, you'll be extremely reluctant to take that risk. Scarcity thinking makes you fearful, cautious, tentative, and tightfisted. It leads you to downsize or outright abandon your vision. It turns you into a brown cow, when in your heart you are a purple cow.

Failing Forward

Years ago, Frank and I, along with the other partners of the practice got the brilliant idea of developing a business within our practice called "Bounce Forward." The idea was to create positive psychology products that helped promote resiliency and healthy relationships. It was actually a pretty good concept, and we hired a top-notch director to lead it. We were still in the development stages when she announced she was pregnant and would need to step down. We were a bit bummed, but we hired another woman to take her spot, who, though she was also extremely bright and capable, in retrospect, did not fully understand the vision of what we were trying to accomplish. After a year or so of limping along, we shut it down. All tolled, we lost about $60,000.

Gulp!

Are we glad we lost 60 grand?

No.

Would we do it again?

Probably.

We share this with you to make a few points. First, even if you take a big chance, you might fail. Even with a good idea and a successful start-up, it may still lay a goose egg. Second, and more important, it may still be worth it. We love basketball legend Michael Jordan's quote, "I have missed more than 9,000 shots in my career. I have lost almost 300 games. On 26 occasions I have been entrusted to take the game winning shot … and missed. I have failed over and over and over again in my life. And that is precisely why I succeed." Jordan adds, "I can accept failure. Everyone fails at something. But I can't accept not trying." And this is our point. We cannot ensure that your vision will be a complete financial success; there are way too many variables in play. But, speaking for ourselves, we would want to be glad that we at least tried. We hit a home run with Southeast Psych, and we struck out big with Bounce Forward. We have at least one other business venture that went belly-up and cost us about $16,000, and we don't regret it at all. We want to be clear that we are not wealthy people with a ton of extra money to sling around. We took out a low six-figure loan to start our practice. We are not impulsive or reckless. Others will attest to the fact that we tend to "move with deliberation." However, we like to dream big and make an impact. Colin, one of John Green's (2008) characters in *An Abundance of Katherines*, sums it up when he says, "What is the point of being alive if you don't at least try to do something remarkable?" Dave has the quote on the desktop of his computer to remind him, because, seriously, what's the point? Even if he fails, he wants to at least know that he at least tried.

This is Dave's seventh published book, but some of his best writing has never found a publisher. The best book he ever wrote was rejected by a couple of dozen publishers and still sits unread on his laptop. But although he has had success with writing, it has been the failures that have spurred him on and sharpened him the most. It's a familiar feeling among writers because no one knows more about failure than they do. As J. K. Rowling has said, you have to be free to fail in this world. In his best-seller *The Alchemist*, Paulo Coelho wrote, "There is only one thing that makes a dream impossible to achieve: the fear of failure." But we like Jack Canfield's pointed quote from *Chicken Soup for the Soul* best: "Everything you want is on the other side of fear."

Smart Risks

A while back Dave was seeing a young man for therapy who had bombed out of college with only four classes left to complete his business degree. As he neared the finish line, his anxiety got the better of him, and he choked. He stopped going to class. He lied to his parents for weeks, and then didn't return their phone calls for the last month of the semester. Understandably, they insisted that he take out a loan to complete his degree. He agreed and got the loan approved a few months later, but then at the last minute, he bailed on returning to school. That's when he came to counseling.

"I'm just scared that I'm going to repeat what happened the last semester," he told Dave.

"That's certainly a risk," Dave responded.

"And then I'd be out with $12,000 with nothing to show for it."

"You've got a pretty big dilemma: decline the loan and don't finish college or take out the loan and take a risk that it may not go well again."

"I know. It sucks. I just read this week that a college degree increases your earning potential by an average of $17,500 every year."

"So a somewhat risky $12,000 investment that might yield $5,500 in the first year . . ."

"And then $17,500 every year after that," said the business major, completing the thought.

You won't be surprised to learn that he did accept the loan and returned to college and completed the degree. The truth is, though, he might have returned and failed again—or never returned at all. But the only way to get the good outcome he wanted was to take the risk.

As you read the story, weren't you rooting for him to take the emotional and financial risks? We're rooting for you to do the same thing.

It's Okay to Make Money—and Okay to Lose It

There's an almost universal experience that most therapists have had in graduate school. They got the message that it is wrong—almost repugnant—to want to make a lot of money in their chosen profession. They hear that to want to make a lot of money or to be motivated by money borders on obscene. And the weird part is that hardly anyone can remember any professor actually saying something like this directly. It's almost as if this message gets into us unconsciously. No one says it, but we all feel it; we all sense it. So let me say what needs to be said: It's okay to make money in your dream practice. In fact, it's okay to make a lot of money.

We don't think it's a great idea for your main motive to become rich, but if you execute your vision well and it ends up yielding a lot of revenue for you and others, then great. This is a true win–win. You serve clients well and bring something powerful and original to your community and, at the same time, you reap the financial rewards of this.

The other side of this is true as well. In a weird sort of way, abundance thinking shows you it's not only okay to make money, but it's okay to lose money. And, trust us, there are a lot of different ways to lose money. You can lose money by making business investments that don't pay off (as we certainly well know). You can also lose money by losing referrals (as we described earlier). There are as many ways to lose money as there are ways to make it. The point, though, is that money should not be your primary motive. The execution of your vision should be your motive. This doesn't mean you should be loose with your money, of course, but it does mean that money really serves the larger mission.

We track each of our referrals with a number of variables: age and gender, who referred them and for what, the zip code, and so on. Over time we can see trends that help us be strategic in our marketing and innovation. When we analyzed the data over a several-month period, we found a pretty shocking statistic: We lost about half of our referrals! That's right. Of all the calls from prospective clients, only about 50% to 60% actually ended up coming in for even one appointment. Why? Some were scared off by the cost (we aren't on any insurance panels, and we charge a decent rate for our services). Others just decided therapy was not for them. For some, the problem got better on its own (often called "the waiting-list effect"). A few others ended up seeing someone else sooner. For those who had financial constraints, we almost always offered the option of seeing a doctoral intern or a younger therapist who was just starting a practice. Even still, our "capture" rate was about half.

There are a few lessons intertwined in this. The first is that there is, indeed, a lot of business out there. Unfortunately, many people who need your services never find their way to you—or to anyone else, either. Only a fraction of the people who need what we offer ever get it. The second, and equally important point, is that it's okay for you to lose business. To be honest, I would love to have a higher capture rate for our referrals because it means that more people have access to our services. But none of us is losing sleep over this. Instead, we realize that losing referrals is, in many ways, a good thing for us. The clients we end up seeing are usually a really good fit for our therapists. They are highly motivated, more collaborative, and tend to see more improvements. Many of our therapists have worked in a variety of other settings—from community mental health to college counseling centers to other private practices—but the consensus is that they have never had better working relationships with their clients. Three months after coming to work with us, one of our colleagues told us, "I absolutely love my clients." We know the feeling because we feel the same way. We don't get hung up on whether we are losing referrals. Instead, we focus on getting the clients who fit each therapist best. Doing so works for everybody. The client wins; the therapist wins.

Scarcity thinking leads to taking what you can get and even taking on clients that might not be a good match for your skills and interests. Abundance thinking makes you okay with losing referrals so you can focus instead on finding your dream clients who are part of your dream practice. This is true regardless of specialty area. We have fellow clinicians who have built dream practices by specializing in seeing individuals with borderline personality disorder, eating disorders, attachment disorders, complex trauma, forensic issues, and other really tough issues some clients face in their lives. For some therapists, these people and their challenges might wear them out, but for the right therapist who has good training and strong inclination, these individuals are perfect clients. If a particular type of client (diagnostic issue, age, gender, etc.) or modality (individual therapy, couples counseling, group therapy, etc.) energizes you, then go for it. Think in abundance terms, not scarcity. Think laser beam, not shotgun.

At Southeast Psych, we had one year when we lost money ($20,000 of loss during the economic crash of 2008), but otherwise, we have been profitable. That being said, our profit margin has been relatively low over the years. Why? Because we have a really nice place with a video studio, a coffee shop and bookstore, and a big support staff. We get good people and pay them well. But all of that serves the purpose of furthering our mission and values. Year after year, we have reinvested in the business to get it to the place where it can fulfill our mission and embody our values. Along the way, we have lost some money in a variety of ways, but I am certain that we have been successful largely because we have been willing to take risks and attempt some new things. Some of those ventures worked well; some of them bombed terribly. But we would not have been willing to do any of it if we did have a healthy dose of abundance thinking. Scarcity thinking would have had us frightened into paralysis, as it did for Jay and many others. Abundance thinking isn't synonymous with the belief that we will always make a ton of money or have huge profit margins. Instead, it is the notion that there is more out there than we have tapped into or figured out how to access.

Years ago when we decided to make our waiting area into a coffee shop and bookstore, we approached Diane to be our manager. At the time, she was serving as one of our front office staff, and she'd made quite an impression on us with her fun and gregarious personality and her hospitable nature.

We were all a bit shocked when she declined the offer.

"We think you'd be great at it," I said.

"Thank you," she said, graciously. "To be honest, though, I just don't think it will fly." She was referring to the bookstore. We understood her concerns. A bookstore and coffee shop in a waiting area of a psychology practice didn't seem likely to make big bucks.

"Well, *we* aren't sure it will fly either, but we are less interested in it making money than we are in it offering a special experience for our clients. Even if it doesn't make money, we are still going to keep it running for the foreseeable future."

She smiled. "If that's the case, then I'd love to do it."

That conversation was almost a decade ago, and she is still managing our coffee shop and bookstore. To be honest, we haven't made much money on that venture, but it has been one of the keys to our success. As we've already shared, that place is a special experience for all of our clients. It is immediately disarming, comforting, interesting, and fun. It's been well worth the investment because it has furthered our mission, regardless of whether it has been a big moneymaker by itself. We never would have done it if we hadn't thought in terms of abundance rather than scarcity.

Scarcity thinking says, "It's too risky." Abundance thinking says, "Maybe it's not risky enough."

Invest in a bookstore that loses money but creates such a special experience that it makes clients eager to keep coming in? Sounds like a good investment to me.

Sink cash into a fully staffed studio that makes videos that people can watch for free online and doesn't generate a dime of revenue but creates tremendous buzz for the whole practice and its therapists and furthers our mission in a powerful way? Sounds like a good idea.

So let us say it again: It's okay to make money, and it's okay to lose it. We've lost some money in the short run in ways that have probably made us the most money in the long run.

Don't Worry About Your Neighbor

Years ago, we had a psychologist in town who asked to have lunch with us. She said it was just to connect with us, but as the lunch went on, it became apparent that she was concerned about our plan to open another office in her neck of the woods. We told her we were very non-competitive, wanted her not only to survive but to thrive, and repeated our mantra that "rising tides lift all ships."

"I'm just worried you are going to come gobble up all my business," she said.

We remember being so jarred by what we were hearing that we weren't sure how to respond. We had no desire to run her out of business. We had always believed there was enough business for everyone. Yes, there was certainly a bit of Darwinism involved. Therapists who weren't very good or had no aptitude or appetite for marketing were probably not going to do well. But for skillful clinicians who were willing to do what it took to connect with others in the community, the sky was the limit. We have long said that if another strong practice opened up directly across from our entrance, it wouldn't raise our blood pressures in the least. This isn't because we think we'll likely run them out of business, but because we think we'll both do well. And if that happened, we would be happy. Knowing us, we'd be thrilled that we had more playmates and more practical joke targets.

As for this woman who was afraid we would gobble up everything, as best as we can tell, she's doing well and our second office is doing well. We have yet to gobble up all the referrals in the area. We know this because we recently had lunch with another psychologist who has an office within a stone's throw of ours. He is not on any insurance panels, charges slightly more than we do, and has a waiting list. Not only were we thrilled to hear this, but we also snagged him to come do an in-service training for us. After that training, several of us referred people to him. This guy is not our competition; he's our friend and ally—and we are his.

Along these lines, never ever bad-mouth your competition. Not only because it's bad form, but because your perception of them is likely to be incomplete and probably inaccurate. Because of the nature of our work, we usually have very little data to make these kinds of judgments. Just because you have had clients come see you who had a bad experience with someone else probably means very little. Those same therapists have probably seen clients you used to see. That's the nature of our work. The fact that someone left another therapist to see you doesn't mean you are a better therapist, nor does someone leaving you to see someone else mean he or she is a better therapist. Much of our work has to do with goodness-of-fit, relationship, and timing. Don't get too puffed up—or too deflated—by this. Always take the high road and refrain from saying negative things about other helping professionals. Instead, wish them well, not only with words but in a heartfelt way.

So don't worry about your neighbor, either whether they are encroaching on your territory or whether they are doing better or worse than you. That's just ugly scarcity thinking. Instead, collaborate with neighbors and support them. It's not only better business, it's a better way to be.

There's a Lot of Need Out There

Not too long ago, one of Dave's college-age clients was telling him how he really wanted to understand himself better before he returned to school. He had bombed out twice already and was just baffled about why this had happened.

"I wish there was someone who could help me figure out my learning style and how to make it work in college instead of just giving me a bunch of test scores and numbers," he said.

"I have just the person for you," Dave said. At the end of the session, Dave marched him down the hall, and introduced him to Craig Pohlman because this is exactly what Craig does.

The following week, Dave had the mother of one of his high school guys seek his advice about her daughter, the client's older sister. She had apparently been hiding an eating disorder for a while and now was in need of serious help.

"I don't know who to go to," she said. "Our whole family needs help with how to cope with this." Dave gave her the names of Lauren King in one of our offices and Heidi Limbrunner in the other, both of whom specialize in helping families successfully manage eating problems.

These people literally walked into Dave's office needing to be pointed in the right direction to get the help they needed. For these two, the help was a few yards down the hall. For others, they might have to be referred to another practice. But either way, a great amount of need is out there. There is no scarcity of need and no lack of work to be done. The issue is not how to scrap and scrape for the little potential business that exists out in your community, but rather how to get some of that enormous potential business out there to find you. With abundance thinking and a willingness to connect authentically with your community, you probably will.

II

Making It Your Own

four

Niche Down

"Hi! I serve clients of all ages. I do individual, family, couples, and group therapy, and also do psychological testing," said a random, forgotten psychologist.

This might be a somewhat exaggerated quote, but these words are not too far away from actual pitches we have heard. This individual suggests she can be all things to nearly all people. It's true that working as a generalist might potentially result in a fairly good practice. However, we do not believe this can lead to a dream practice. Instead of trying to be everyone to everybody, we encourage clinicians to specialize, or "niche down," on who you are, your experience, and what you are passionate about.

In retrospect, many of our supervisors over the years seemed rather broad in their specialties. Their practices tended to be general, especially if their private practices were a side act to their main career. While Frank was on internship, he was immersed in research studies, bureaucratic meetings, and tested by the trials of residential treatment serving kids struggling with conduct disorder and reactive attachment disorder. These were great and tough years, and he enjoyed close relationships with many supervisors who were all therapists in one form or another. His regular contact with these clinicians and quasi-mentors allowed him to know more about their careers and how they created their professional lives.

Nearly all of these individuals had a private practice. They shared bits and pieces of their private practice lives, but not enough for Frank to understand the process by which they built their sideline businesses. The business and creation of a private practice seemed like an unknowable secret. Frank loved being there and learned a great deal, but an opportunity arose in his home state of North Carolina that he could not refuse. And so, after 3 years, he returned to North Carolina to join a private practice. Yes, he was licensed and had proven himself clinically and professionally among his peers. But he had essentially no concept of what a private practice looked like or how it functioned, much less how to start one. His image of private practice remained ingrained in what he had seen on television or in the movies.

When Frank thought of his supervisors and other psychologists during internship, he did not think to ask, "What was their niche?" To him, a niche meant things like child psychologist, psychoanalyst, cognitive behavioral therapy, and so on. He pretty much assumed, once you were a therapist, your niche was defined by the age or broad categories of people whom you served. When clinicians are asked what they do, answers are often, "I'm a school psychologist," "I'm a social worker," "I work with adults," or "I serve all ages." While spending time at Devereux as a staff psychologist, Frank wanted to grow up and be a "child psychologist." Whatever that meant . . .

So in the late1990s, Frank moved to Charlotte, North Carolina, to work with Dave and join a small private practice. Other than Dave, he knew nobody, had no referral contacts, and was pretty much terrified. This practice had a 60/40 percentage split. Out of the $105 hourly rate, he would get 60%, and the rest went to the practice. For that percentage, appointments were scheduled, charts were prepared and filed, and other administrative tasks attended to. Frank actually had to float between offices back then and had no dedicated space. He also had to provide his own computer and various supplies. This was all brand new to him. There was no manual on how to build a private practice. He was left with the "hang out your shingle and hope the phone rings" philosophy.

Dr. Lynn Vivian, who gave Frank his first job in private practice and to whom he is always indebted, encouraged him to take any and all clients. If the presenting problem was a little outside of his specialty, the instruction was to receive supervision and training in that area and broaden his experience with a greater variety of clientele.

Therefore, he took on learning disability evaluations as well as evaluations for attention-deficit/hyperactivity disorder (ADHD). But he also took on clients struggling with anxiety and panic attacks, along with children in the midst of divorce. At that point in his life, he was "hungry" and needed to find ways to pay the bills. As such he worked with a wide variety of clients but stayed within his broad range of training, which was essentially child/adolescent psychology with family systems theory. That became his niche.

New postdoctoral candidates and interns at our practice are still encouraged to follow this model but with an enhancement. Yes, new clinicians should try to take on enough clients within their scope of training to "pay the bills," but they should immediately begin considering their niche. This niche is what will define and distinguish them to their community and colleagues. To encourage this process of professional identity, these newly minted professionals go through our mentoring process. Through this year of weekly mentoring, clinicians define their niche and learn how to build their own dream practices.

When clinicians come into the practice or when people are figuring out how to develop their dream practice, we encourage them to really ask what they could be the best at and where their passions truly lie. We also explore the economics to see if their passion and skills could viably lead to their own definition of financial success. We argue that it's best to be specific and not have five or six different niches. We ask each clinician, "Where can you drill down to be your best, and will that actually pay off?"

Knowing your passion and skill makes connecting and serving easier. Saying, "I work with ADHD, depression, couples, and families, oh, and I also run a group for teens" does not sound especially unique or special.

When you communicate your message in a general, "cast a wide net" fashion, you are selling yourself as a generalist. Instead, we encourage young professionals and early career therapists to think along the following lines:

1. Take all referrals for which you feel professionally competent.
2. Have both a short- and long-range vision and process to develop your niche(s).

Think about this: Are you more likely to remember that therapist you met who specializes in complex trauma or the one who said he sees all issues and ages? More specifically, if someone tells you Asperger's is awesome and you need to know why, will her name resonate more than the person who says, "I run social skills groups"? If you cannot communicate your niche, you are not the purple cow people notice and remember.

Niche Conversations

We want clinicians to understand and fulfill their dream practice vision, but to do this, we need them to actually think this through specifically. One of the first questions we ask in mentoring a new clinician is "Describe your dream practice." Many times, there can be a long pause at this point in the conversation.

Often there are vague answers about working with adults who are struggling somehow with life. Often we hear, "I like to help kids." Rarely do we hear a well-thought-out niche and dream practice concept. This is true even among seasoned clinicians.

In reality, important tasks do get in the way of true contemplative thought about what one's dream practice would look like. For years, clinicians in training with an eye on private practice have been focused on someone else's research, spending innumerable hours on a dissertation, applying for internships and postdoctoral fellowships. And don't forget the hours and hours of studying to get licensed. What time was there for thoughtful, ongoing discussions about private practice?

We know that we never really spent time sitting and thinking about what our real and concrete goals were going to be. Informally, Frank's relationship with Dave over the past two decades has allowed for such conversations. And in turn we create a space to help clinicians spend time and articulate their niche(s), which should combine their passion, skill set, and economic viability. Find a way to simply and articulately communicate your niche. Let's take a look at car companies as an example of niche expression as well as marketing and experience.

Typically, when you see a commercial for a lower-priced car, the advertisement lists many of the features of the car. The announcer states, "This car comes fully loaded with air-conditioning, power windows, a 10-year warranty, and heated side-view mirrors." He lists all of the things that come with the car to make it sound like you are getting a lot for your money.

Now think about the commercials you have watched for Mercedes or BMW. They talk about the experience of the car but rarely list the car's features. Why is that? The argument seems to be that if someone is seeking a high-end product, you would assume good features, high-quality, and a unique experience would be standard. If someone is seeking a lower end product or a less expensive service, that person tends to check carefully about the list of features and options. BMW and Mercedes have created brands that require little explanation; they have created a niche.

What does this have to do with being a clinician?

We argue that therapists do not need to overexplain what they do or how they do it. You do not need to say you do individual, group, and family therapy. But you do need to be able to clearly articulate your niche, and, as we stated earlier, the "why" you do it. What is your passion?

When you consistently connect with the communities you want to serve, the topic of specialty or niche will always come up. But before entering into a relationship with these communities, you must have some idea about what your niche is and how to express it without resorting to the "I do therapy with people" line.

That first question from a colleague or community connection is usually, "So, what do you do?" This is your first opportunity to express your niche and distinguish yourself as a purple cow. Frank's niche answer to this question is, "I'm a psychologist, and I love working with Aspie kids and families. I am trying to help them feel like superheroes, help them find friends, and deal with feeling different." He does not say, "I'm a child psychologist who does individual, family, and group therapy with Asperger's kids."

Those answers may sound the same, and both answers are true, but the first answer expresses his niche, his passion, and shares an emotional experience. It also leads to a deeper conversation. He wants to connect people to his interests as well as learn about theirs. Niched clinicians tend to be more readily identified, and their names come to mind in connection with their expressed passion.

Try this exercise. Think of a few topics (e.g., autism, parenting, marriage, ADHD), and see if names, locally and nationally, pop into your mind. In our dream practice, we can name an individual for most specialized areas. It's actually amazing and exciting to see more than 30 clinicians in our group who are all building their dream practices. They are doing what they love and what they are good at doing. But they are linked to their niche(s) in a way that makes them memorable. That's what a niche does.

Therapists who specialize in a particular area often find their names rise to the surface above the buzz of all the other generalist therapists. This is not to say that a psychologist cannot create a generalized practice and be successful. This is especially true in more rural or underserved settings. However, the ones who seem to be the most satisfied with their practice and are more successful, both in terms of quality of life and financially, are the ones who find and promote their niche. To find your niche, you must take time to think about it in a deliberate fashion.

Niche as a Special Experience

We can't say this enough. Finding a niche will distinguish yourself in your community and will make you more recognizable. At Southeast Psych, most clinicians have clearly delineated niches. One of our close friends, Nick Valadez, started as an unpaid intern. He also worked with a well-respected ministry and connected with the corporate executive community on both national and global scales. Nick is constantly learning and has created a niche serving couples as well as highly stressed corporate executives. He has also created a special experience for people who come to see him.

In helping people become more organized and live more deliberate and peace-filled lives, Nick has created an office that exudes peace and organization. When Frank wants to rest a bit and take a breath, Nick's office is one place he will go. He has created an office that provides a niche experience. He did not seek out the stereotypical therapist's office. Nick's office colors are soothing, and he created a comfortable and simple seating arrangement. His desk is always clean and organized. There is no clutter. He also customized his shelving so the light from outside shines through his ordered book collection. There is the fun touch of a few action figures here and there, but the order of his office allows for rest, peace, and thought. He created a space that fit his practice and his clients' needs, and thus his office experience is unique. As in the car commercials, a niche can include a special experience, and that is how we describe him to our friends and clients. In essence, Nick is kind of his own brand, and that brand fits his passion and skills but is also economically viable.

Maybe you have heard that Starbucks coffee strives to become America's "third place." We have our home, our workplace, and then . . . Starbucks. We would say they succeeded. Caribou Coffee strived in a similar fashion, and based on our weekly visits and attempts to find a seat on the crowded leather sofas by the fireplaces, Caribou has succeeded as well.

In our practice, we have created our own niche experience. We strive to break down the stigma of therapy and to actually make seeking help and support a fun experience. We have achieved this special experience in a variety of ways.

While writing this book, the Olympics were on our 60-inch flat screen TV. Our waiting area was attended to by our hostess, Diane Balcer. Diane and Frank meet each week to discuss how to make all of our clients, young and old, have a special experience. We have "Throwback Thursday TV Land" when we show old television shows such as *Happy Days* and *The Munsters*. We also have movies based on fun holidays. During December, we probably show the movie *Elf* 100 times. Diane also teaches our knitting club, initiated by Dr. Heather Wright. This club builds community for some of Dr. Wright's clients and has dramatically enhanced their lives.

Furthering the special experience, Marti Flowers, our amazing office manager, decorates our waiting areas as well as the back hallways and offices in elaborate detail based on seasons, holidays, or special events, such as presidential elections, the Olympics, and Valentine's Day. We could go on and on about the special experience we try to provide for our clients and even our own therapists. Southeast Psych's niche is taking care of our clients by offering a Fun, Innovative, Relational, and Excellent experience (FIRE—remember, this is our acronym!). Certainly our style is not for everyone. This is our dream practice. You are building your own, much in the same way that each clinician builds his or her own niche. We have our niches, and you have yours. Frank's niche and approach to Asperger's may not be yours. In his office are Ultimate Collector Lego Sets from *Star Wars*, comic books, zombie memorabilia, and *Star Wars* models hanging from the ceiling. He also has a big flat screen TV and Xbox prominently displayed.

Frank's community and niche includes Aspie kids and their families. In 17 years, he has never had a kid not talk with him on some level therapeutically. He attributes this to a match between his passionate niche as well as learning how to communicate this through a special experience. Seeing the sign outside his door that says, "Star Wars Way" makes communicating his niche and experience even easier.

Be Willing to Say No

To build your dream practice, you cannot be everything to everyone. To have your dream practice, you do need to be able to say, "No." Having movie posters in the hallways, superhero-themed caricatures, and movie days may not be what some clients or therapists are looking for. Being secure in your practice and knowing that you do not need to create the movie stereotype of a private practice can allow you to say no to clients who do not fit. It also allows you to say no to colleagues who do not understand or appreciate your vision of your dream practice.

In the beginning, you need to be able to buy groceries and pay the rent. You also do not want to practice outside the scope of your training. For most of us, our training was rather broad. In Frank's case, he received training in school psychology when based in school systems in a rural North Carolina county. He also was supervised and trained in child psychology within hospital and residential programs. Later, he received specialized training working with adults who were dually diagnosed with intellectual disabilities and mental disorders such as schizophrenia. That's some pretty broad training! And because of his training, he was able to accept many of the referrals that came through the door in his first few years of practice. But to be able to build your dream practice, you must be willing to say "No."

Dr. Andrea Umbach is one of the many awesome psychologists at Southeast Psych. Andrea was either lucky or determined to figure out her niche while she was in graduate school. She had a clear vision of the communities whom she wanted to serve and began pursuing those clients while on internship. Andrea specializes in the treatment of hoarding, trichotillomania, obsessive-compulsive disorder, and anxiety.

She knew her niche early on and drilled down on that specialization. She also had the self-understanding to know what age ranges she serves and connects with best. Andrea is an example of someone who has expressed her passion for a particular area of private practice and has communicated it so well that she is years ahead in developing her dream practice. If we get a referral for trichotillomania, Andrea is the only clinician to whom we will refer. Because her name is linked with her specialty, we think of her first.

If a referral for behavior problems or bipolar disorder came specifically to Andrea, she would often, if not always, say no. Within our group practice, as well as the greater community of clinicians in Charlotte, Andrea is able to send that client to another clinician who has a better match in terms of a niche. In the short-term, the decision to pass this referral to someone else cost her billable hours. Remember, she needs groceries too. In more literal economic terms, at her hourly rate, she probably declined $3,000 of personal income over a year of treatment.

That is a lot of money to say no to, especially when first building a practice.

By declining some referrals, Andrea is becoming distinguished as a psychologist who has a niched practice. The communities with whom she connects know her now as someone who specializes in a specific area related to the broad spectrum of anxiety. Her specialties are not mood disorders, ADHD, or parenting. Yes, she can serve such populations, but to build her own dream practice, she will need to say no to such referrals.

There is a relational aspect to niche building as well. As a result of sending a referral to another colleague either within or outside her own practice, Andrea is further viewed as generous and someone who is connected with the idea of providing excellent care. Andrea's name and passion are linked to her unique specialty. She knows who she is and is building a niched practice that reflects her passion.

Through her connections within the anxiety treatment community locally and nationally, word has spread. She now has her first book contract and is also a blogger for the *Huffington Post*. She is the prototype of a clinician who has identified her specialty and has communicated that well to the community she serves. Her result is a thriving practice and a recognized niche linked to her name and to the broader brand of Southeast Psych.

Broadly speaking, when you have colleagues within the same practice or within the same community who are communicating, cooperating, and finding their niches, everyone benefits. By saying no to a referral and directing a client to another clinician who has a needed niche, you are communicating the recognition and value of the other clinicians' specialties or special experiences. We do not think in terms of competition with other clinicians or practices. Trying to compete does not build healthy relationships or experiences and will not result in a dream practice.

10,000 Hours

In his book *Outliers*, Malcolm Gladwell (2008) examines what allows someone to have extraordinary success. One concept that appears repeatedly in his book is the idea of "10,000 hours." It basically means what it sounds like. If you drill into a specific task for 10,000 hours, you might become an expert at that particular task or endeavor. It's not true in all areas, but it can be true in business. It can be true in sports. It's certainly true in private practice.

When new clinicians come to Southeast Psych, we often assume they know a lot more about therapy and practice building than they actually do. We hear it said that it's good to surround yourself with people smarter than you. If that's the case, Dave and I are definitely surrounded. However, the difference between smart and successful tends to be the test of time. Experience really does matter. But even younger clinicians can build their dream practices if they are willing to put the time and effort into it. Most clinicians are intelligent or they would not actually have made it to licensure. But with that said, despite exceptionally high IQs and university pedigrees, it takes a great deal of hard work, self-reflection, and effort to build your own dream practice.

We have put in well over 10,000 hours into building our dream practices. We cannot imagine spending 10,000 hours working in a field in which we don't have passion and skill.

Make your niche match your singular passion and your skill set. Build your dream practice around a specialty you love. Then be the best in town in that one area. Make it your niche. Own it. But don't forget the 10,000 hours.

five

Connect With Your Community

Your training is now complete . . .
—*Darth Vader*

So are you ready to hang up your shingle yet? In the past, that word *shingle* was used in a variety of ways, but it typically described how a doctor, lawyer, or some similar professional would take an extra tile left over from the construction of a roof and hang it on a pole in their yard or above their entrance. The tile was usually slate, so people could write on them with chalk to advertise their name and business. Starting a private practice now sounds pretty easy: Find an office, hang out a sign, and some guy will knock on your door for help.

Right?

Well, maybe there's a little more to it than that. Maybe you need to get that website done, create an e-mail address, and set up a phone number. Also, maybe throw in a few professional memberships to national organizations, place an ad in the newspaper, and perhaps add a few extra bucks for a bold-font ad on the Internet under "Psychologist." Oh, and don't forget your business cards. Now, with everything in place, that guy is bound to start knocking soon.

Right?

Insert sound of crickets chirping here.

So when's that guy going to start knocking on your door? Will he show up just because you want to help people and he saw your ad on the *Psychology Today* website? Sure, you have a strong and noble desire to improve lives, solve big problems, and help people become fully actualized. You are a therapist, for goodness sakes! Maybe you've been sort of like a therapist your whole life. Maybe you were the kid whose friends told you all their problems. Or maybe you had a really rough childhood and are inspired to prevent difficulty in the lives of others now.

No doubt you have a lot of good reasons to be in the profession you have always dreamed about. And to be in this profession, you have sacrificed. Good grief, have you sacrificed! Years and years of school, tuition, delaying the start of a family, and maybe even the loss of relationships due to your passion to help others. And now that you've hung up that shingle and created your web page, you can tap that passion!

Right?

That guy still hasn't shown up.

It's now dawning on you that there are maybe a few more ingredients in the secret sauce of dream practice success. Well, thank goodness for all your business and marketing training. Yes, now is the time to be thankful for the business courses you took, as well as all the employee management courses and the accounting classes. Those courses taught you how to think about business and explained in detail how to negotiate a lease, gain lines of credit, successfully resolve employee conflicts, and—here comes the really, really important part—how to market and brand your dream practice. Now, as they say in business, "Your enterprise can now be fully deployed and engaged with your customer base."

You did get that training, right?

Right??

Yeah, neither did we.

Almost certainly you have the skills to do your dream job and the passion to really help people. No doubt you are hungry to serve and care for others. But now, maybe you are realizing you have the skills to be a good clinician but lack the skills to make this contraption fly. How frustrating is it to know you have the skills to help others, and at the same time, you can't actually use those talents?

All too often we have met with young clinicians, or even more seasoned clinicians, who don't have a clue how to tell the world—much less their local community—about their desire to serve and care. These outstanding clinicians, while putting on a brave face, are scared and frustrated. But they admirably try to get out and meet local referral sources such as schools, churches, and doctors in their offices. In reaching out to their local community, they often revert back to their training and indoctrination. They are ready to give an answer to that all-important first question everyone must apparently care deeply about, "What's your theoretical orientation?" And, of course, they know the answer to this question! They figured it out through all the externships, internships, practica, and hours upon hours of clinical supervision.

But have you ever wondered why you are asked about your theoretical orientation in those internship interviews? Does it tell you what kind of clinician someone is or whether he or she will be able to build a practice? Does any real person in real life ask those questions? That boilerplate interview question about theoretical orientation is simply code for ensuring that you've learned to think in these simple little boxes from the first days of graduate school. Maybe it's based on the traditions of apprenticeship "hazing," but nearly every grad student is asked the question when applying to internships or when being interviewed for an agency job. From early in our careers, we are already being asked to pigeonhole ourselves into one way of viewing the philosophy of our helping profession. And we are also taught through this process that this is how things are done: Think inside the box.

But let us ask you a question: Will the mother of a nine-year-old boy care about your theoretical orientation when she calls your office after his father died in a car wreck?

Will she be asking where you did your internship?

Of course not. She will want to know if you can help her son make it through their family's own personal disaster.

You have trained for years to serve people in their time of need. This family and so many others could use your skills and passion. They need to find you and your dream practice. Building this dream has little to do with your lack of business training or how cool your website looks. It is not especially about your theoretical orientation, but it has everything to do with why you went into the helping profession. A dream practice is about making relational connections that help people. To tweak a political phrase, "It's the relationship, stupid!"

Marketing? Blerg . . .

Frank had been working with a client and their family for about two months. They were focused on parenting and family dynamics to reduce the yelling and nagging that had negatively affected their family relationships. The therapy went very well, and they were wrapping up.

The client asked, "Do you ever do any trainings?"

"Yes, but they are usually more like stand-up comedy routines where I tell a lot of stories," Frank said. He added saying, "Incidentally, this isn't too much different than my actual therapy sessions."

She laughed and asked if he would be interested in speaking to some of her church's Sunday school classes on a few topics.

He said, "Sure! I'd be glad to help."

The mom pitched the idea to her church. The idea would be for Frank to address child development and parenting, which, as mentioned earlier, is how he had helped her and her family.

The next week, the church e-mailed Frank and asked if he would help out. He again said, "Sure!"

The next question was how much would Frank charge to come present. The reply e-mail was the following:

"I would love to help out and please, no payment needed. Glad to help you guys out."

Needless to say, the church took him up on his offer and a couple months later, Frank was slated to give three presentations over three weeks to one of their adult Sunday School classes.

As a side note, by that point in his career, Frank's schedule was so full that he couldn't take on a new client even if he wanted to. In addition, he rarely did such talks on the weekends, and the classes fell on Sunday mornings, which took him away from his own weekend activities and time away from his family. However, for important communities with whom Frank is connected, he will carve out such time. To be honest, he doesn't consider this time spent out in the community meeting people and giving talks to be marketing. This time is purely to connect and serve. The goal was not to go to the church, tell them his name, and ask for clients. The goal was to serve his client's church community and meet some new people. He wanted to help.

But scheduling the presentations did not end there. The good people in these Sunday School classes were not the only group Frank wanted to help. He had another agenda, as well.

Once the talks were scheduled, Frank went to a few colleagues who were new to the profession and just starting to work on building their own dream practices. The conversation went something like, "Hey! I'm giving a bunch of talks at this church and would love for you to come along. I'll be sure to work you into the talk and call you out. If you can come, you can bring business cards but act casual. You are there to meet people and hear their stories, not get clients."

The clear message to our colleagues was that we are going to the church to connect, learn their needs, and be authentic. But the secondary goal was to serve our new colleagues through introductions and, more importantly, to teach them one way to build their own dream practices. It's one thing to tell others how this all works. It's another to show them and walk them through the actual process in person. Connecting and building relationships takes time and sacrifice. So too will your dream practice.

A Hard Lesson: Forget What You Think You Know

And so the first training day at the church arrived. Frank wore his best suit (okay, his only suit). However, not knowing the dress code, he still missed the mark. The church was rather casual, but the suit conveyed respect, if nothing else.

Before heading into the church building, Frank confirmed the names of the e-mail contacts and who asked him to give the talk. He had a backup of his PowerPoint talk as well as a few books to give away as a gift to the individual who had invited him to speak. These are all points to pay attention to when giving a "killer presentation." We will speak more about killer presentations in the next chapter, but Frank's presentations are typically very specific. They are also well-rehearsed, brief, and energetic. Plus, if he doesn't have the audience laughing and thinking that he's quite an odd guy, he has not done his job. But Frank always tries to bring his best presentation every time even if the room has only three people in it. And this happens on occasion.

So on the morning of the first church talk, Frank met three of our colleagues outside who agreed to come along. They goofed around and headed into the church. The room was bigger than they expected and there were a lot of people. The woman introducing Frank started into a very long introduction, which was way more than what was needed. Frank graciously laughed and said, "Don't worry about all that mess, I'm just glad to be here and meet all of you. I hope this information is helpful, but I am also psyched to find out more about your church community." Then he launched into his talk.

Throughout the presentation that morning and within all his presentations, Frank weaves in stories about our colleagues and their work. To a fault, he is self-deprecating but can also use it humorously. He is always the "dumbest guy in the room" as far, as he is concerned. So he elevated his colleagues in a complimentary and respectful way, but with the intent to help the audience hear them as people with whom to have a relationship, rather than as just people to go to for therapy or testing.

In one of the talks with this church, they wanted to know more about Asperger's, so Frank brought along Dr. Kelley Bolton, who specializes in working with Aspergirls. In the middle of the talk Frank said, "You know who else is awesome at this? It's Dr. Kelley Bolton." He pointed her out in the crowd so people could see who she was. With the crowed looking at her, he added, "She is exceptional at working with girls who are on the autism spectrum and has created this amazing Super Girls group that's fun and builds really cool friendships for these girls. It's awesome what she does!"

But Frank wasn't done there. He further added, "But don't judge her, she's from Alabama. Hey Kelley! Don't they have a good lacrosse team or something down there?" The audience laughed. With Dr. Bolton now beet red, Frank further built a connection by noting she went to a prestigious seminary on the West Coast and had a great deal of experience in pastoral counseling. Now the audience knew more about her as a person, and there were some connecting points, including being from the South, potentially similar religious beliefs, and expertise in an area in which they are interested. In just this small exchange, Frank was able to help Kelley build a connection and start a relationship with this community.

But back to that first church presentation with our three colleagues, we can tell you one thing happened that day that was revealing about marketing and why it can feel so yucky for so many of us.

Two of our coworkers stayed after to answer questions and meet people. Frank introduced one of them, Dr. Jessica Bloomfield, and spoke highly of her work with trauma, as well as time she spent overseas in Croatia serving a war-torn population. She very naturally engaged in conversation and learned more about the church as well as the fielding some questions about normal development for teenage girls. This was a natural relational connection.

Our other colleague who was new to the practice and young in the field stood next to Dr. Bloomfield. She was exceptionally dressed, professional, and listened attentively with a bright and natural smile while Jessica spoke with her new "community friends." When the chance arose for him to introduce this other young woman, Frank again spoke very highly of her education but also added some cool facts about where she lived and her impressive background. After this introduction, her answer to the group standing around was, "I'm very glad to meet you. Here is my business card. I work with married couples, do parenting work, and am a graduate of Purdue University. If you have any friends or know of people in need, please have them call my office for an appointment."

Let me pause and say this is not made up or a joke. This was pretty much what she said. We remember it because Frank was kind of in shock at that point. Her self-introduction was blunt and conveyed, "I'm a big deal, I need clients, and this is my business. You are valuable to me if you send me referrals."

That first conversation was about her, not about the individual she was meeting.

The people with whom we were talking politely took the cards, smiled, and then continued their conversation with our other colleague, Dr. Bloomfield. Of the two women, she was the one that genuinely wanted to serve and connect. She was authentic and did not come to the presentation to blatantly display her desire to gain clients. She came across as interested in the community, curious about people's lives, and willing to serve and learn. This is about authenticity, not a sales job.

You cannot build your dream practice without authenticity. Jessica had it; the other woman, not so much.

So why did our other colleague fumble this opportunity despite many preparatory conversations to the contrary? We think it was because she was defaulting to some of the business training she received earlier in her career when she was surrounded by high-powered individuals in the habit of putting their names and cards out in front of as many people as they could. We also think she was anxious at this point and needed clients. Although Frank was frustrated, he also felt for her. We began to get clarity that this individual was not going to be successful in private practice unless there were some dramatic changes in her mindset. Her approach with that group made Frank feel as if his efforts spent working with her were wasted time. She either didn't get it or chose not to get it. After that, she and Frank had many conversations about the culture and tone of "marketing" within the context of building relationships and finding ways to serve a community. People can tell when something is being sold to them. Marketing can feel like car salesmanship, and in a dream practice, there is absolutely no place for such conversations.

As an aside, Dr. Bloomfield now has a thriving practice and helps others in their practice grow their own relational connections. She is a mentor to others and is a hyper-connected individual with many authentic relationships and connections. Our other colleague just could not quite make it work. Her clinical skills were strong. But her ability to connect with others and get outside traditional marketing techniques prevented her from building her dream practice. Ironically, the clinician who could not build a practice was one of the few in our group who had extensive business training. Jessica had none.

Many colleagues across a variety of disciplines have told us that marketing usually feels awkward and fake to them. It feels as if they are subtly, or not so subtly, selling themselves and their services like a drug rep. We've heard people at parties or other social events directly ask pediatricians or other potential referral sources for clients, not unlike the experience in that Sunday School classroom with this overeager young professional. It's bad form, and it's self-centered. Asking for clients and objectifying referrals will not result in a dream practice.

Connect

We've known many excellent clinicians who fail to build a practice because they were overcome with anxiety about getting themselves established in the community. They had resigned themselves to drop-ins, cold calls, and advertising. We've also known average-skilled clinicians build thriving practices because they figured out how to connect with their community.

The key word in building your dream practice is *connect.*

To *connect,* by our definition, is to find ways to match your skill set to the needs of the community around you and then serve that community with no expectations in return. Essentially it means making friends and building authentic long-term relationships.

Authentic means real, of course. We can't emphasize this enough, especially in the helping profession. If you cannot build authentic relationships with a colleague or community professional, you have an uphill battle in building your dream practice. In most towns, there are many therapists, but the ones who rise to the top are invariably the ones who know how to connect on a relational level, both in the therapy room and in the larger community.

"Tell me more about what you are doing," or "I want to know more and understand what you do," are our standard prompts when we meet people and organizations. By nature, we are genuinely curious about others. In building a practice, we need this information about others, what they are like, what they need, how they tick. We can do a better job for our clients because we know these other professionals so well. By dedicating time toward building relationships within the community, we are also serving and connecting with our clients as well.

But when we meet others and build those connecting relationships, we do not enter into this relationship expecting anything in return. If we move into this relationship with other motives, then this relationship building exercise will be seen as fake. Also, we can't maintain a friendship or relationship with someone or a community unless it is real. We just don't have enough energy to be fake. Within these connecting relationships, we hope to learn something new about a person or community and hopefully meet a new friend. We are curious and relational people, which makes this somewhat easy for us, but it wasn't always like that. We needed greater comfort with ourselves. We needed to understand our own quirks. We needed to know who we connected with well, too. It took time, perseverance, and practice.

If you are building your solo or group dream practice, colleague connections are essential. Certainly in a group practice, the most important community of connections is your colleagues down the hall. In the beginning, you will likely get more referrals and knowledge from your own colleagues than anywhere else.

You know the saying "It takes a village." Well, in private practice, we find that it really does take a village to build a dream practice. And in our village, we visit with our colleagues and learn about their lives, their goals, and their dreams. We want to know how we can serve them so they can achieve those goals.

Connecting through serving a community means serving the community of your colleagues and staff as well. Through the process of being present in their lives and careers, you are more likely to be on their mind when a client or training opportunity crosses their path that might be suited to your interests or ability.

If you have an authentic regular connection with a colleague, this relationship in itself can generate referrals. At Southeast Psych, we have a structured yearlong mentorship program (discussed in more detail in Chapter 6). Each clinician who joins our practice has a mentor for a year. This mentor guides the new clinicians and is their "go-to" person for basically everything, including how to build their dream practice. One of Frank's "mentees" was Dr. Kristin Daley. She is certified in behavioral sleep medicine and at one point in her career was the head of a sleep program for one of the largest eye, ear, nose and throat medical practices in the country. When Kristin joined the practice, they met each week to help develop and build her dream practice, as well as help lead the Rest Assured Sleep Program at Southeast Psych, which was originally founded by Dr. Melissa Miller.

Frank has probably only referred 10 people in 15 years to a sleep specialist. This lack of referrals on his part is pitiful especially given many of his clients, many of whom are Asperger's, struggle with healthy sleep. Dr. Daley was consistently on his relationship list, and her name and specialty was obviously more at the forefront of his mind. Since mentoring her, learning about her family, her crazy German heritage, and also her failed attempts at Twitter, Frank has probably referred 30 people to her within 6 months. Learning about her specialty opened his eyes to a resource he had missed and helped him become more attuned to his own clients' needs. This relationship has made Frank a better clinician and has also helped to build Dr. Daley's own dream practice. One thing that is emphasized in her mentoring sessions is for her to get out of her office, walk around, and simply sit down to talk with her colleagues. The more you are seen moving around and present in a practice, the more likely you are to build your dream practice.

One of Frank's favorite professors in graduate school, Dr. Joseph Lowman at the University of North Carolina at Chapel Hill, told him a story about two construction workers. The first was told to work very hard for the whole day at his job and try to outpace all the other workers. A second worker was told to walk around with a clipboard but do no work at all. At the end of the day, all the workers were surveyed on their opinion about who was the hardest worker. The answer? The guy with the clipboard!

This story is not designed to encourage walking around a lot and doing nothing. However, we believe it does speak to the idea that if you are seen and present, you are more likely to be remembered and known. When building a dream practice, being seen and known is a key. This is true throughout the communities with whom you connect but also who you spend time with right down the hall. Don't wait on others to connect. Go and meet them!

Frank knows that he is doing his job when his colleague, Dr. Sean Knuth, says, "It's so weird to see you sitting at your desk and working." Exactly!

An Example of Connecting

One community in Charlotte that Frank cares a great deal for is the Jewish Community and specifically the Charlotte Jewish Day School led by Mariashi Groner. This is an exceptional school with a small budget. He learned of one of their special classrooms for kids who learn differently and asked for a tour. Mariashi graciously gave him a tour of her school.

During the conversation, Frank heard and understood one of her needs. Her school is on a small budget and needed some extra training for their teachers. This was not stated but implicitly understood as he listened to her story and her passion for her school.

As it turned out, Frank is trained to work with teachers within school settings and thought maybe he could help out this school and Mariashi's teachers. He let her know that he wanted to help by offering trainings if she were ever interested.

We've not discussed our first meeting, but we imagine she might have been thinking Frank was there under the ruse of trying to get referrals. Frank stuck to learning about her and the school. Following up later, he emphasized that if she wanted to take him up on the offer, she should feel free to call or e-mail him. He gave her his personal cell phone number, asking her to not share it with anyone. But he wanted her to know that he was making himself personally available to her and her school. He was truly impressed by what he saw and would not have offered his services if he did not feel passionately about what this school was attempting to do.

A few weeks later, Frank got an e-mail and a call. She stated that she wanted some help for her teachers on assertiveness and communication skills. He offered to come and do a couple trainings. He prepared for the trainings so that he would give an excellent talk and also to demonstrate the value he placed on this relationship. And thus, we began our connected and long-term friendship. That first training led to talks about Asperger's, interpreting psychological reports, parenting strategies, and a variety of other topics.

Since his introduction to Mariashi and the Day School, Frank has become super-connected to the Jewish community. The community has invited him and our practice to participate in large, nationally recognized conferences with the likes of Barbara Coloroso, author of *The Bully, the Bullied, and the Bystander*, as well as Lee Hirsch, the director of the nationally recognized and prize-winning documentary *Bully*. Mariashi and her day school even allowed us to use her school bus for a trip our practice took to the American Psychological Association convention in Washington, D.C. We have also been able to offer reduced fee services for some of her families who were in need, and our trainings continue to be offered to her and others within the Jewish community in Charlotte free of charge.

Just that one day of reaching out through curiosity and interest about a local resource, as well as offering to serve, has built a lasting friendship. Through this friendship, the Jewish community of Charlotte has learned that there is a psychologist in the Bible Belt who legitimately wants to help and serve. Of course, this relationship did actually result in innumerable clients over the years, but that was not why Frank built the relationship. He is always thankful for the clients that he gets to work with, but even if he never received a single client, he would still maintain service to that community. Connecting in this way demonstrates selflessness and humility and has helped to build Frank's dream practice.

We connect because we are genuinely interested, not because we want anything in return. To that point, Frank gives between 15 and 20 presentations throughout the year through our Super Speakers brand (www.thesuperspeakers.com), and he gives all of the local presentations for free. In a typical year, Southeast Psych clinicians give between 150 and 200 free presentations.

Dr. Trey Ishee, a colleague and good friend, gave us a valuable tip about fees for presentations. Often a school, church, or other group will offer a check at the end of the presentation or mail a check after the talk has been given. Dr. Ishee suggests signing the check back over to the organization and requests that it be given to a charity or donated back to the organization itself. The idea is to continually communicate to your communities that you want to connect and build a "selfless" relationship with them. However, we will tell you, it is fun to get the occasional gift card to Gamestop or Target. Those do not go to charity.

If you shift your thinking to connecting relationally and stop thinking about "selling your services," building your practice and reputation feels much more natural and authentic. If you are reading this book, it is likely you are in the helping profession. Get back to your passion and start thinking of "marketing" as another way to helping and connect. That's why you are a therapist.

Right?

Do this and clients will find you rather than you going out to find them.

six

Market Relationally

When we first started out, we probably knew more about string theory and particle physics than we did about marketing. And we know essentially nothing about physics. Over the years, through lots of reading as well as great conversations with colleagues like Mary B. Moore, someone legitimately trained in marketing, as well as social work, we have built a consistent model of marketing that is linked to how we connect relationally.

As we discussed earlier, connecting with your community is vitally important to building your dream practice. The theme of relational connecting permeates our message. Think of the places you frequent, like coffee shops, restaurants, and the local gas station. Most of these locations are brands, and you develop your own relationships with them, especially the more frequently you visit.

Think of brands such as Microsoft, Starbucks, or Disney. People build relationships with these brands. Dave is attached to Apple, but Frank is a diehard PC fan. He built a relationship with Microsoft in the '80s by learning how to program using MS-DOS. He still remembers a lot of that programming and can work his way around a PC very well. We each have a relationship with these brands and, as you know, relationships are not entirely logical. Relationships exist on an emotional level.

Frank loves his local Caribou Coffee Shop. Why? Because the guy who prepares his coffee knows him, which coffee he wants, orders before he asks, and remembers his name. He also loves the trivia questions to try to get 10 cents off his coffee. As the song from the TV show *Cheers* says, they are a place "where everybody knows your name." There are many Starbucks (or other coffee chains) that do the same, but the Caribou here in Charlotte reached out to Frank first. He is now loyal to them.

Frequent contact facilitates a relationship. Think about our colleague introduced in Chapter 5, Kristin Daley. She was on Frank's radar, and, as a result, a seemingly new whole area of need—sleep disorders— became increasingly present in his mind. His referrals to her multiplied. The relationship is legitimate and reciprocal. The relationship is marketing—especially in helping professions.

The Marketing Model: Little m and Big M

Let's think about marketing in two ways, "little m" and "Big M." The little m stands for mentoring and the Big M stands for Marketing/ Branding.

little m

As mentioned earlier, for their first year, new clinicians at Southeast Psych are provided a mentor. This mentor is not necessarily someone who shares their same area of expertise. He or she must possess the qualities of a strong mentor. In Tony Dungy's (2010) book with Nathan Whitaker, *The Mentor Leader*, he argues that good mentors have specific traits. Having a mentor who approximates Dungy's description of a leader allows for a relationship that looks very much like that of an apprenticeship. There are many versions of a mentor and many traits to be found in such a successful relationship, but an underlying theme is clear. Tony states, "The key to becoming a mentor leader is learning how to put other people first. You see, the question that burns in the heart of the mentor leader is simply this: What can I do to make other people better?" (p. 5). The apprentice is put first. Finding relationships that serve as an apprenticeship experience can radically accelerate the development of a dream practice.

Through a mentoring relationship, the message and culture of your dream practice can be sharpened and shared. For an early-career clinician or someone fresh out of grad school, the role of the mentor is to help instill and model the culture and vision of a practice. If you are in a group or solo practice, finding a good mentor can make a huge difference. Division 42, the independent practice division of the American Psychological Association, has created a mentoring program for clinicians across the country. Your local professional organizations may have a mentoring program. Find one that has demonstrated a clear passion and drive to help individuals in private practice thrive. As a profession, we are realizing that a big component of success—if not the biggest—is having a strong mentor.

In his book, Tony Dungy writes about mentor leaders in depth. He examines the traits of these individuals and offers qualities someone would hope to find in a successful mentor. Not everyone should or can be a mentor. But if you are looking for one, based on the descriptions in Tony's book, you are looking for someone who is authentic and secure in his or her own skin. You are also looking for someone who stays focused on the mission at hand and helps hold you accountable to your goals, from the little steps to the giant leaps that go into building your dream practice.

Specifically, good mentors perform a variety of tasks, including introductions to communities and individuals, writing letters of endorsement, and maintaining and preparing for weekly mentorship meetings. These weekly meetings cover everything from helping to create an individualized marketing plan to knowing where good restaurants and schools are located. The formalized and consistent tasks in this relationship are valuable.

Invaluable, though, are the relational activities mentoring can bring. These may include little things, such as bringing a mentee coffee, remembering a birthday, and getting other colleagues to notice him or her by joking around. The job as a mentor leader is to give some of our new referrals to them, even if that means we may a have a couple empty slots that week. Our goal as mentors is to put our mentees first—to make them feel valued, excited, and connected to the culture of a dream practice. The mentor is the new clinician's point person, and the weekly face-to-face meeting is the key to maintaining momentum. A successful mentorship almost invariably leads to a successful dream practice.

For later career clinicians, mentoring serves all of these same functions. However, the mentor relationship can also serve to help unlearn some of the messages picked up from their training and earlier experiences. One inhibiting message could be "It's bad to make money at this job; I do it because I care." Another might be "I need to have a couch in my office with a water feature to sooth my clients." Or even, "I need to do therapy in my office rather than on a horse farm." This message may limit how they see their practice and future.

Dr. Melissa Miller is a good friend and joined Southeast Psych after having been a leader in her own successful group practice for 5 years. Why did she join us? First, she speaks highly of her old practice and her colleagues there. All dream practices are different. As we say often in this book, our dream practice may not be your dream practice. Her reasoning was she wanted her own dream practice, and to do this she needed tools that Southeast Psych could provide that also fit her personality.

Frank first met Dr. Miller during her postdoc year at a Southeast Psych open house costume party. He had a temperature of a 102 (and no, he didn't know it at the time) and was dressed up as a "Clown Pimp." (Yes, sad but true.) Someone took a picture of him that night, and just over his shoulder way in the distance, was a tiny photo-bombed head. It was Dr. Miller looking at Frank like he was a crazy person (or that she was crazy to even be there that night). They stayed connected over the years mostly around their mutual love for Harry Potter, but it was more of a peripheral friendship for the two of them.

As a mentor, Frank took two of our clinicians to lunch to meet with Dr. Miller and help build a relationship with her because she had become the president of our local psychological association and was also a prominent member of the local community. During that lunch, there was brainstorming, laughing, and sharing all of the fun stuff that was happening at Southeast Psych. She showed genuine enthusiasm and interest in all the things happening at our practice. Our meeting that day was all about connecting and learning what was happening in each other's practices and lives.

As they talked, Frank realized again how fun she was and how great it was to talk to her. Halfway through the meal he blurted out, "Why aren't you working at Southeast Psych?!"

Her answer was, "I don't know Frank, you tell me."

Six months later, Dr. Miller was a clinician at Southeast Psych and was the brand creator and leader of Rest Assured, one of the coolest sleep medicine programs in the country. Dr. Miller was drawn to our Blue Ocean way of thinking. But it all began with a friendship around Harry Potter. Southeast Psych is full of these stories of relationship building and a can-do attitude. As you think about your own dream practice, consider your own connections and how you can facilitate greater relationships. You never know where these relationships can lead. Marketing is relating! Dr. Miller was one of Frank's mentees and is an example of "little m" marketing.

Mentoring is a method by which you can overcommunicate your internal message. It provides a space to cultivate culture and allows for a way to remain connected to how people are doing. Mentoring also holds people accountable to the goals of a dream practice. Creating your dream practice is possible without mentoring, but it's a lot tougher and a lot lonelier. At Southeast Psych, the formalized process of the mentorship, or "little m" helps further our brand.

"Big M"

The process of marketing and branding the visuals and culture of a practice is what we call the "Big M." How you do Big M should develop out of a conversation that defines your mission and core values. Once this culture is defined, the method of branding and marketing your dream practice becomes clear. Big M can fall into the more traditional stereotype of marketing and is what we all think of when it comes to a brand. Examples are the cursive script of Coca-Cola, the three-pointed star emblem of a Mercedes, or the mermaid from Starbucks.

Marketing who you are or what you are doing creates value by helping your clients connect with you emotionally. As you think of companies such as Marvel, Google, and Disney, what mental images, emotions, colors, or memories do you conjure? When Frank thinks of

Disney, his mind goes in many directions—all of which are awesome. He thinks of video games, *Star Wars*, superheroes, rides, television shows, movies . . . you name it! But he feels happy when he thinks of Disney. (It is the happiest place on Earth after all.)

When you begin to develop an emotional connection, or rather "an experience" with a company or even an individual psychologist, you have built a relationship. Building a dream practice has a lot to do with marketing and branding through the Big M process.

Let's take a look at how we built and marketed the brand of Southeast Psych.

Southeast Psychological Services

What's in a name? The first practice we were a part of before starting Southeast Psych was called Morrocroft Psychological Group. The name actually made a lot of sense and worked. We were essentially a boutique South Charlotte private practice near the upscale Morrocroft neighborhood. We really enjoyed our work at Morrocroft and learned a great deal about what it meant to be a psychologist in private practice. Although we weren't formally working in such a manner, Dave was Frank's mentor in that job.

We were very thankful for the opportunity at Morrocroft, but that exact model of private practice was not our idea of a dream practice. And, at the time, there was really no way for us to have known that. We really didn't know, what we didn't know. There was no manual for building a dream practice back then.

When we were first thinking about naming our new practice, our examples were really just what we had seen in other places. While brainstorming names, we thought we would be creative and think of the Southeast as our future community whom we wanted to serve. And yes, even then we were thinking "the Southeastern United States." We did not want to limit our scope right from the start. But our conversation began with location.

After carefully thinking all this through (which took about an hour), we settled on the name, spent $50 on a logo, and picked the color "Carolina Blue." We both graduated from the University of

North Carolina at Chapel Hill and had the audacity not only to color our logo Carolina Blue, we also thought it would be a great idea to paint all the offices in our new space the same Carolina Blue that was in our logo.

In April 2000, the new brand and dream practice of Southeast Psychological Services was born.

Evolution of Southeast Psych

As the years passed, we had many brainstorming sessions. Brainstorming at that time involved group and individual conversations across every layer of our practice. Receptionists, seasoned clinicians, and interns were all included on some level. We always try to encourage people to think big, be creative, and not compare our ideas to other businesses in the world. Encouraging a Blue Ocean way of thinking requires legitimate brainstorming sessions where ideas can be shared and not judged. All ideas are considered and honored. Through honest and direct conversation, new ideas and passions that reflect your interests can bubble to the surface. In this way, dream practices can be built.

Direct and creative conversation within brainstorming sessions can result in lots of ideas—some crazy and some pretty awesome. But how can you tell which will work and which will further the marketing and development of your dream practice?

In the book, *Great by Choice,* Jim Collins and Morten Hansen (2011) shared powerful examples of how companies prepare deliberately for change and growth. They offered an example of how Microsoft would throw out a few new ideas and ways of doing things to see which ones would stick or gain a little traction. Microsoft has failed on many ventures and new ideas. But the argument is that they have succeeded more often than they have failed, because Microsoft is deliberate in its strategy.

The analogy from *Great by Choice* was that of firing bullets rather than cannonballs. Bullets are cheaper and allow you to find your target more accurately. Once you have found your target with a few bullets, that's when you fire your most expensive cannonball. Bullets are cheap;

cannonballs are expensive. This model is in opposition to just building a cannonball based on a few ideas and firing everything you have.

Microsoft was in competition with IBM for operating systems way back when. IBM spent lots of money on a cannonball operating system, but at the same time, Bill Gates was spending "bullet money" or less expensive ammunition on a competitive operating system called Windows. Some people within Microsoft were against Gates's idea, but given the limited resources being spent, the project continued. When IBM's cannonball system failed to sell and testing proved Microsoft's bullets were accurate, Gates built a cannonball and fired. I doubt you are working on an IBM operating system right now.

As a group, we have fired a lot of bullets and a few cannonballs. Brainstorming and trying out a few ideas without knowing what will work is not only okay, it's encouraged. Listen to your own private brainstorming sessions or sessions with colleagues and friends. Then try a few out. If you find a few things that start to work within your own marketing and branding efforts, then build your cannonball and fire!

Southeast Psych and Our Cannonballs

Through brainstorming sessions, Southeast Psychological Services was changing, growing, and moving in directions we had never dreamed of. Brainstorming resulted in our own cannonballs, some of which we've already discussed:

- A new mission statement that connected to our core values
- Creation of brands (Mind Matters, Mind Over Body, Rest Assured, etc.)
- An actual publishing house (Hero House Publishing)
- Having free conferences for the community
- Building a bookstore with a hostess who cared for the waiting space and offered free coffee and tea
- Having big flat screen TVs to show movies and TV shows that reflect our brands and mission
- Providing a children's waiting area with an Xbox 360 and model rockets hanging from the ceiling

- Placing superhero themes with life-size superhero figures everywhere, superhero caricatures of each clinician, a comic book as a brochure, and superhero movie posters
- Building a video production studio
- Developing a second location
- Creating an Association of Psychology Postdoctoral and Internship Centers (APPIC) internship site

Some ideas worked, and some did not. But within a year or two of creating Southeast Psychological Services, it became crystal clear that we would be providing more than services. The nice little name for our business and all the Carolina Blue no longer reflected who we were or what we were doing. Our logo and our name no longer reflected our brand. The initial Big M thoughts of April 2000 limited our scope and vision and did not reflect of our culture. Plus, it's kind of hard to be emotionally connected to "Southeast Psychological Services." That's like saying, "I really like eating at the Ronald McDonald's House of Hamburger Provisions." McDonald's is a way better name. Mickey Dee's is even better.

So we pivoted. It was time for a redesign and reimagining of how we were branding ourselves and our message. Through this process, we retained the name "Southeast" but shortened it to "Southeast Psych." We considered changing the name entirely, but because we were already well known at the time, logic suggested we retain some recognition in our community. Had we to do it all over again, the name probably might have been something like our tag line, "Psychology for All" or maybe even, "The Purple Couch!"

So with a new name, we needed a new branded logo. This was professionally designed by a graphic expert who researched our field, knew us relationally, and understood our culture. John Jung is the logo designer for all of our brands. He taught us many lessons through this process. One of the more valuable lessons was, "A child should be able to draw and recognize your logo." He asked us to think of McDonald's and Starbucks and visualize the simplicity of their brands. If your hand can create it, your mind can remember it.

John understood we wanted to transform our practice as well as the perception of psychology to everyone on Earth. Yes, Earth. (We prefer to think of ourselves as ambitious instead of delusional). He also understood we wanted to get psychology into the hands of as many people as possible to enhance their lives (our mission statement, yet again).

John Jung immersed himself in all of the superheroes and movie posters in our offices, experienced our culture and humor, and engaged in a relationship with us. Instead of $50 for a logo, we spent $1,000 for a logo from someone who was an expert and was able to help us convey the emotion and simplicity needed to build a true brand. And with this newly formed Big M, we could create a truly brand-loyal experience for our clients and community.

John, through a lengthy and important series of conversations, moved our logo into the genre of the hero, and in so doing, created the iconic "S" logo which you can find on all of our branding materials. We are known for the "S," and people have emotionally and relationally connected to the brand.

Now armed with our new name, mission, values, and logo, Southeast Psych was able to communicate much more clearly and move into the "how" and "what" of our dream practice. All of the brands at Southeast Psych move through this same process. The visual branding (Big M) is just as deliberate as the relational (little m). Marketing and branding is based not only in the look of your logo and the message you convey, but also in how you share this image and culture with all of your communities.

Share Your Dream Practice

Once you have established your mission and have a name and logo, it's time to start thinking about how you will share with the world the exciting news that your dream practice has been born. There are innumerable ways of spreading the word, and in the years ahead, unknowably more methods will emerge. There's the classic trifold brochure, the pen with your phone number and website engraved on the side, or the mug that has your logo on it. There are also hundreds of

social media outlets (Facebook, Twitter, Reddit, etc.), local community events to attend, radio and television, internet banner ads; the list
could go on and on.

At Southeast Psych, we used some swag and a little advertising,
but honestly, not that much—probably far less than other companies
our size. Many practices do mass mailings, have mugs or fliers, and, of
course, don't forget the business cards. Sometimes people order these
products with their name or brand on them because it gives them the
tangible sense that their practice exists. And that's okay. But creating
marketing materials or swag is just one minor tool within Big M branding. And putting your name on a pen is really just that. Everyone does
it, but it does not make you the purple cow.

Thinking about brochures, swag, and social media should only
begin once you have clearly articulated the mission of your practice.
When thinking about your mission, the populations with whom you
want to connect become clear. And as a result, the physical materials
or other methods through which you communicate will gain clarity.

The tagline we want the world to see is "Psychology for All." The
community with whom we want to communicate our mission is "All."
And by all, we definitely mean everyone and everywhere. Within the
vein of connecting and branding everywhere, Southeast Psych strives
to build relationships, and we market our relational connections literally all over the world. From the Middle East and our relationship with
our dear friend Dahlia Abbas (an Aspie mom and mother to two spectrum boys in Baghdad, Iraq) to Tania Marshall, the author of *Aspiegirl*
who resides in Australia and spreads the good news of strength to
Aspergirls everywhere.

Sharing your brand and marketing your practice may be dedicated
to just a local community, or it can be focused globally. Either way
the same principle applies. Build relationships that are authentic and
reflect your specific interest in helping others.

Mission and Values Define You

Although external branding and marketing is important, guiding
principles need to drive these efforts. We use our mission statement,

core values, and tagline as our guiding principles. Our acronym, "FIRE," which stands for Fun, Innovation, Relationships, and Excellence, allows us the framework to think through our marketing efforts. All of our branding and marketing can focus on communicating our message consistently and effectively using FIRE as a guiding principle. The consistency of our message through this acronym can be seen in our print ads, our online presence, and even our T-shirts, mugs, pens, and all other kinds of swag. The culture of a dream practice should match well with all your branding activities. If you see Southeast Psych swag or media, you will recognize our consistent themes.

Think again about coffee mugs. We remember our very first one. It was back when we still had the Carolina Blue logo and our name was Southeast Psychological Services. But that first mug made a lasting impression on our community because it embodied the process of our acronym. On one side of the mug was our light blue logo and practice name; on the other side was our website and in quotes the phrase, "We put the 'fun' in dysfunctional."

Although some people could have been offended by this phrase (and some were), most loved it. Within a dream practice, it's okay if people don't agree with your approach. Seriously, you don't need to get everyone's approval. Remember, the haters are gonna hate. Most people in our community seemed to appreciate the levity that the little phrase brought into their lives. It was fun. Most importantly, the communities whom we sought to serve got it. Anyone can go and get a mug or a pen made with their information attached. But how often are marketing materials crafted within the helping profession with a fun and inspiring mission behind it? We would argue that very few people have engaged the practice of therapy in this manner. Because you are reading this book means you are beginning to think about your dream practice in a different way.

An Example

Our Rest Assured behavioral sleep medicine brand provides services focused on difficulties associated with sleep. This seems obvious, right? Like most other programs, they have a classic trifold brochure that is informative and shares the usual bios, pictures, and programs that are offered. But you can also find the fun and innovation in the brochure as well. During their brainstorming session, the team thought outside the box. Imagining sleep, dusk, and how to demonstrate their concept visually, the team came up with many awesome ideas. The result of their process included the "gift of sleep" gift card for newborns and their moms as well as a fun Twitter account to share sleep facts. Also, within the brochure they created, you can see the fun the team had in putting this together. For the cover picture, they hauled a large bed down to a pond and put it on the dock. The image is fun and also conveys the culture of Southeast Psych, but also the Rest Assured brand. They have mugs as well but included with these mugs are a spoon and a bag of Sleepy Time tea. It would have been far easier, cheaper, and more straightforward to just create an informative flyer or trifold brochure. But the team asked themselves the important questions. How are we making our brand fun? How are we being innovative, excellent, and relational? The answers to those questions helped to drive and create the marketing materials they needed to fulfill their own mission and brand.

So how do you market and build your dream practice? Is it about swags and slogans and signs?

Not so much.

Marketing is more about relationships. It all begins with your mission statement. When that's clear, it all shifts to relating authentically and consistently to others. Mentoring relationships are especially critical. If you are in a group practice, find your mentor. If you are a leader, find your mentees. Solo practitioners can find mentors, through friends, former colleagues, professors, or professional organizations that support your profession. These relationships are the absolute key to your marketing efforts. And through the little m process of mentoring and accountability, you can develop your Big M plans.

III

The Scary Stuff

seven

Present Powerfully

The Ignite movement has taken root, and now there are dozens of these evenings in major cities around the country. The premise is simple: Give a five-minute talk on your area of expertise featured on 20 slides that auto-advance every 15 seconds. Once you start talking, the slides begin, and there is no stopping it. If you mess up or your mind goes blank or there is any other major or minor calamity, you just keep plowing through. It's like a runaway train.

Craig Pohlman, the CEO of Southeast Psych, had been selected to present at an event called Ignite Charlotte. Craig must have drawn the short straw because he was the first speaker of the evening. He had no chance to scope out the other speakers or size up the crowd. He stepped up in front of the audience of several hundred people and confidently began his talk. He's a learning expert, having written three well-regarded books on helping children succeed in school, and he picked the topic of memory, which, ironically, was a good choice.

He was cruising along perfectly, and then the screens went blank. The slides just vanished. The perils of being the first speaker of the night were fully realized. At this point, we would have called out for brown pants, but Craig just kept trucking. Our minds would have been racing: *Are the slides still auto-advancing or have they stopped? Will the screen ever come back up?* Craig just kept on his pace. A few long seconds later, the screen came back up and they were exactly in sync with him—or rather, he was exactly in sync with them. It was a mini-marvel. He went on to give one of the best talks of the night. Craig, along with Frank and Heidi Limbrunner, both of whom also gave great presentations that night (Heidi only a week after giving birth, by the way), made us all proud that evening.

What struck me about Craig's experience, though, was that it wasn't great by chance. It was great despite the obstacles and land mines—the technology failure, the time constraints, no notes to rely on, and an unfamiliar and eclectic audience. It was the product of practice and experience and real effort to hone the craft of speaking to an audience. There are a few "pure shooters" out there (to borrow a basketball term)—individuals for whom public speaking comes naturally with little practice or effort. For most of us, we get good at it when we do it a lot and keep refining it.

There's little question that one of the keys to building your dream practice is giving great presentations in your local community. But just because you are a good clinician doesn't make you a good presenter. In fact, based on our experiences at conferences and workshops, it seems most clinicians are actually lousy presenters. Recently Dave was in New York for a high-profile two-day national conference that pulled in some of the best clinicians in the country, and in his judgment, more than half of the presenters were subpar. One woman, a talented and accomplished clinician, literally spent an hour reading her PowerPoint slides word-for-word. The frustrated man beside me leaned over and said, "Can you believe this? That's something you learn not to do in Public Speaking 101."

The truth is that most therapists never get Public Speaking 101. We are taught how to do therapy but not how to communicate therapeutic principles to a mass audience. As a result, we see a lot who retreat to the safety of reading their slides verbatim and others who are just scared to death of speaking to a crowd. If this describes you, you're not alone. A major study found that fear of public speaking was the one feared above all others, more than spiders and snakes and enclosed spaces. It was the one feared more than death itself. As Jerry Seinfeld once joked, "At a funeral, the average person would rather be in the casket than giving the eulogy."

So you may be scared to death of the idea of public speaking, but it is often an essential part of building your dream practice.

Therefore it's a skill set you need in your tool kit. By nature, most clinicians are in their offices all day in one-to-one or small-group meetings. If you do a good job, these clients will send others your way. But you'll probably need a greater referral base to build a viable practice, especially at the beginning. The best way we've found to spread the word to a lot of people quickly is to give good presentations. Trey Ishee, one of the leaders of our Super Speakers brand and himself a gifted speaker, says, "If I give a good presentation at a school, I'll get six or more referrals the following week." Trey gives his talks for free with no expectation of return, but the truth is, when you present well, you can't help but get referrals. You connect with your audience and meet some of their genuine needs. They see your personality and your expertise on display, so, of course, many of them will want to work with you. Even if they don't, you have still served them well and met an important need.

One of the themes of this book is to put fear aside. For some, public speaking challenges that notion like nothing else. We hope there will be plenty of information in this chapter to equip you well and encourage you to step up to the mic.

Before You Open Powerpoint

Years ago when Dave first started giving presentations, he would get the topic and start creating slides based on information that he knew, random thoughts he had, and research he could access quickly. He would create slides without regard for where he was going or where he wanted to land. He just wanted to get the content down so he could shape it up. The approach was to get the block of granite on the table and then start chiseling away. After he had a bunch of slides, he would begin to arrange them, throwing out some, adding a few others, until he had what looked like a solid presentation. Most of the time, the talks went well, but there was a little something missing. He realized it was what Simon Sinek shared in his well-known TED Talk: It wasn't *what* he was talking about (facts, stories, and so on), it was *why* he was talking about these things. The why is as important in giving a talk as it is in starting the practice itself.

It's easy to focus on what you are going to talk about and then spend your time on crafting your slides and focusing on your content. It is harder to step back and ask yourself why you want to give this talk. Ideally, you are not giving the talk to get referrals. Those are just the byproduct of a talk well conceived and well delivered. And you also aren't giving your talk just because someone asked you to do it or because you know something about the topic ("Dave, could you come talk to our staff about managing stress?"). No, you should be giving a talk for a deeper reason and a higher purpose. To get there, ask yourself two questions before you create that first slide:

1. *Why do you care?* Notice there is an assumption in this first question. It assumes you care. It assumes you are emotionally invested in your talk. So if you aren't passionate about it, maybe you shouldn't be giving this presentation. Seriously. But assuming you do care about it, begin to articulate to yourself exactly why you are drawn to this subject. Dave developed the "Eight Traits of Great Parents" talk because he believed parenting is a skill set that we can all get better at with some encouragement, equipment, and practice. That's the spine of the talk. Does he care about this topic? Yes, a lot. And he knows why he does. Before you give any talk, make sure it's not just a topic you know but something you care deeply about. It will make a world of difference.

2. *Why should they care?* So it's great and essential that you care about the topic but you also want the audience to care. Why should they care about what you have to say? For Dave's parenting talk, he thinks they should care because he has practical ideas for becoming a better parent. For his "Truth About Teens" talk, it's because he has up-to-date facts about teenagers that will help parents and educators understand their kids better. When you are clear about why they should care, it helps you develop your talk in a way that informs your conclusions and applications. You identify the need you are trying to meet (greater skill, good information, encouragement, and so on) and then you construct your talk to meet that need. Essentially, you are also answering the question, "What problem is my talk solving?"

Simplify the Presentation

Once you answer these questions, you can move on to laying out the presentation itself. Assuming you are going to use some sort of visuals, which is typically a good idea, it's essential to do this well. The rule of thumb is that you want simple visuals without much text. We have many older presentations that are just full of bullet points and text. They contain a lot of content, but they are visually busy and crowded. They pull the audience member into reading the slide rather than following us as speakers. As a result, there will be less attunement and connection with the audience members individually and as a whole.

We've gotten increasingly better at simplifying our slides. We favor using an image that helps the audience remember the concept with only a few words or a brief phrase per slide. What this forces us to do is to know the talk really well, rather than being like the woman in New York who simply read us her slides. We have to know the content thoroughly. As a result, the slide reinforces what we are saying and makes it stick in people's minds. The simpler and more visual, the more sticky the content will be.

You'll probably remember that one word and one image more than if we had a ton of bullet points with great material, right? When it comes to the visuals, simpler is better. As you are laying out the presentation, write good notes—perhaps even draft the whole things longhand—but make the actual slides very simple with only images and a few key words or phrases.

It's possible to give a good talk without strong visuals. Some storytellers, preachers, and politicians do it all the time. However, when you are giving a presentation with a good amount of content to digest, visuals are usually pretty important.

The best way to do this is by using software presentation packages. We know there is a movement in some circles to move away from PowerPoint or Keynote slides, but we're not on that bandwagon. We find them to be immensely helpful. When done well, these presentation packages can really enhance your talk in at least five key ways:

1. They give the audience visuals to go with your audio. Coming in through both channels helps them to remember the content better.
2. A well-done presentation package signals that you are well prepared for the presentation and that you take their time seriously.
3. It forces you to organize your content better.
4. It allows you to give the talk without other notes, freeing you up to better engage the audience. While you don't have all the content on each slide, they serve as cues or reminders for all the other information you have in your head.
5. It sends the message you know your stuff.

Your slides should be elegant, visually appealing, and simple. There should not be a lot of text or multiple graphics. Instead, they should be elegant and striking. To do this, consider these guidelines:

1. Each slide should typically have only one to three keywords or phrases at the most.
2. Use one picture per slide (although there can be some rare exceptions).
3. Use at least 28- to 32-point font.
4. Use simple, nondistracting backgrounds.

PowerPoint is an excellent piece of software that keeps getting better with each version. However, Dave is a Mac guy and has grown to love Keynote. If you have the chance to use it, please consider it. The learning curve is a bit steeper, but the payoff is higher. The transitions are more exciting, and the versatility is astounding. Prezi is another presentation software for both PC and Mac that is well worth your time to learn. In Prezi, the whole presentation is on a giant digital canvas and you can dive down into it or roam around to different locations on it. It's a visual marvel and especially effective when used well. You can use any of these packages to create strong visuals for a remarkable presentation.

Connect With the Audience

Like being a good therapist or a good basketball player, being a good speaker is a skill that requires both training and practice. You didn't get to be a good therapist without training and practice, and you won't be a good speaker without them either. But, like therapy, public speaking is at its best when it is a relational experience. In therapy, we become attuned to a client; we adjust and find different rhythms with different individuals. Presenting to an audience requires a great deal of attunement as well. But to get there, we have to practice our material so well and know it so completely that we can focus on the audience and not ourselves. Practice not only the phrasing but rehearse the transitions and choreograph your big movements.

Assuming that you have done a good job of practicing, when the time comes to deliver the talk, approach it more like a conversation than a performance. Your tone should be authentic. They should get a glimpse of your personality. It should be you up there in front of the audience. Back to our basketball metaphor, if you practice all the mechanics—dribbling, passing, throwing—then, when it's game time, you don't have to overthink it. You can just play. The same is true for speaking. You practice it to the point where you don't have to stress about the delivery. You get freed up to make an authentic connection with your audience.

Begin and end your talk with a punch. It needs to start strong. It also needs to end strong. We cannot overstate the important of practicing your opening and closing. Do you remember learning about "primacy and recency effects" in Introduction to Psychology? Most people will evaluate your talk based on the opening minutes and the final minutes. Although this might seem nerve-rattling, it's actually liberating because it lets you focus a lot of your mental energy into a very manageable task: craft a short introduction and closing remarks, then practice until you know it cold. We advise you to have a three-line introduction that involves the following elements:

1. Your name and affiliation
2. Your topic and structure
3. Your introductory hook

Using this simple structure, this is how one of our talks might start:

1. Hi, my name is Dave Verhaagen, and I'm a psychologist with Southeast Psych in Charlotte. **(Name and affiliation)**
2. I'm going to talk with you tonight about Eight Traits of Great Parents and I'll share the eight qualities that the very best parents seem to possess—and how you can develop them yourself. **(Topic and structure)**
3. Recently an older mom told me that despite raising four kids into adulthood, she was always scared she was going to make a big mistake and, in her words, "screw up their lives." **(Introductory hook)**

So what makes for a good introductory hook? Admittedly, this is a matter of personal bias, but having coached dozens of presentations, given hundreds ourselves, and sat through thousands, we will give you a short list of what to consider. First, let me tell you what I would *not* do:

Don't Start With:

- **A definition**—*"Webster's says the definition of conflict is . . ."* Automatic snooze.
- **A cartoon**—"And then Beetle Bailey says . . ." Creates distance and feels stiff.
- **A group exercise**—"Let's all stand up and . . ." Perhaps the most annoying of all. I came to hear a competent speaker not have some team-building moment with three random people.

Those three starters hardly ever go well. At best, they are benign; at worst, they are off-putting and the audience starts feeling like this is all going to be a colossal waste of time. But now for the good stuff. Since Dave is a child and adolescent psychologist, these are a few examples of how he might start his opening hook.

Try using:

- **A short story**— *"Mark was only 12 years old when he started drinking . . ."*
- **A fascinating question**—*"Are kids today more violent than they used to be?"*
- **A surprising fact**— *"The average teenager spends 53 hours a week in front of a screen."*
- **A striking quote**— *"Gertrude Stein said, 'Everybody gets so much information all day long that they lose their common sense.'"*
- **An eye-catching visual**— *"If each marble in this jar represents a child, this is how many children report being abused each year in this state."*

All of these are relatively quick, but they tend to be effective because they stir both thought and emotion. In *Made to Stick*, Chip and Dan Heath (2008) advise you to grab the listener emotionally by using good stories, unexpected twists, and simple, compelling ideas. It's good to do that right off the bat. You probably know for yourself that you begin to size up a speaker very quickly. If you can come out of the gate strong, you have a much better chance of hooking your audience. Once that happens, stumbles and fumbles in the middle of the talk will be easily overlooked and forgiven.

Once you have given your brief introduction and your opening hook, it's good to use what is termed an *advance organizer*. An advance organizer is succinct information that you provide to your listeners before presenting your main points, allowing them to mentally organize and anticipate the flow of the presentation. For example, following an introductory story, Dave might say, "Tonight I'm going to give you eight traits that seem to be true of great parents. These are eight things that the best parents do well. I'm also going to show you how you might be able to put these traits in practice in your own parenting." Simple as that. The listener now knows the basic structure and flow of the entire talk.

Now you are well into your talk. The audience members are form-ing their impressions of you, so you want to make that early connec-tion. Think about a time when you heard a really outstanding speaker. What was it that made him or her so excellent? No doubt the content was good and helpful, but my guess is there was something more. If you break it down, it probably had to do as much with the nonverbals as it did with what was said. The speaker probably had that ability to look at members of the audience and perhaps even physically move toward them in ways that made a connection. You would be wise to emulate those skills for your own presentations.

This means you look them in the eye, give them a warm smile, and have a tendency to linger on one person at a time when talking. It's a conversation. It's a connection. Use your face well. Especially when you are speaking before a large group, your facial expressions and ges-tures have to be a bit broader than they are in a one-on-one conversa-tion. You have to smile and scowl and puff out your cheeks. One of our interns complimented Dave on a presentation, saying, "I realized you really are performing. It's still you, but you are definitely performing a little bit." That's absolutely true, and we admit it unapologetically. Often the best presentations have a bit of theater in them. They are not necessarily over-the-top, but there is a little showmanship involved. You don't do it to showboat; you do it to make a connection between you and your audience. You can have a sense of performance and still be authentic. You're just using your face and your body a notch more expressively to span the distance between you and your audience.

Eye contact is so important. As basic as it seems, many presenters fail to do this well. They seem like they are in their own world, discon-nected from the audience in front of them. Sometimes this is due to inexperience, but mostly it's due to nerves. If you get nervous when you speak, imagine you are having a conversation with just three people: one on the left, one on the right, and one right in front of you. Pick a receptive face in each of the three locations—someone with good eye contact, preferably smiling or nodding—and lock in. Talk directly to that person. This accomplishes two things: First, it calms you down and makes the task of being up in front of people more manageable, and second, it helps you make a connection with your audience. Once you feel comfortable with these three receptive folks, begin to take in more people with your eye contact and gestures. By the end, see if you can connect—if only for an instant—with everyone in the room. At your best, each member of the audience should feel like you are talking to them personally.

Depending on the setting, it may also be a good idea to get out from behind the podium and move closer to your audience. Don't roam around just to be moving, but use your movement as a way to make a point or keep interest. For example, if you are talking about two contrasting ideas, you might move to one side of the room for the first side of the argument, then shift to the other side of the room for the other. Sometimes you need to stay planted in a single spot for one reason or another, but when you have the freedom to move, do it strategically. Either way, always strive to use your face and body to make a strong connection with your audience.

Throughout your talk, keep the connection with your audience by telling good stories. Dave likes to tell personal stories about his own experiences as a dad, a husband, a therapist, or just as a human trying to get through life well. If he talks about his wife or kids, he gets their permission first. If he talks about clients, he always disguises the details in a way that would make it impossible to figure out who it is. But Dave likes real stories of real people. In his parenting talk, he shares both his triumphs and failures and uses these stories to evoke emotion in the audience. He wants people to feel something because when they feel it, they remember it. It sticks with them longer. And the stickier, the better.

Let us give you an example. Dave is an incredibly squeamish person. The sight of blood nearly makes him nauseous. Even stories about injuries—especially injuries to the fingers or eyes—almost lay him out. He can hear psychological gore all day and it doesn't do him in, but one cut finger and he's down for the count. When he was a teenager, his uncle told a story during a car ride about how he accidentally jammed a screwdriver into his eye while trying to repair his wedding ring. Dave came close to passing out just hearing him describe it. Even writing about this makes him a little tingly. So when he had his own children, one of his greatest fears was that they would have a bloody injury and he wouldn't be able to be as good a dad in that moment as he would need to be. That day came when his oldest daughter was about 10 years old. She was upstairs cleaning a glass aquarium that she was using as a hamster cage. She had dumped the dirty bedding into a trash bag, but some of it was stuck to the bottom of the cage, so she flipped the whole thing upside down and was thumping it hard with her bare foot.

Thump! Thump! Thump! Crash!

Dave heard shattering glass and immediately jumped off the couch and sprinted upstairs like someone had plugged him in to an electrical outlet. He was up there in three seconds flat. He flung open the door to her room and saw her leg stuck in a pane of jagged, broken glass. Her foot was bloody. It happened so fast, she hadn't even had time to start crying. She just looked at him with terror in her eyes.

Dave slowly pulled her leg out of the glass pane and picked her up and carried her to the bathroom where he sat her on the side of the tub and began inspecting her cut foot for shards of glass. He found a piece about the size of postage stamp and pulled it out with his fingers. He washed off her foot and wrapped it, then got her into the car and to the urgent care where they got her stitched up.

It wasn't until later that evening when he was processing it with his wife that he realized he never faltered for a moment. He sprang into action. He held the bloody foot and pulled out the piece of glass. Such a thing was almost unthinkable to him before he had children. Now it was just something he did without a moment of hesitation. And that's how it is when you have kids. Your love for them overwhelms your own hang-ups and neuroses. Your desire to protect them is stronger than your fear.

You can probably see where Dave could go with this in a talk, but let us ask if you felt something while you read that story. Did you feel stirred by it at all? Do you think you'll remember it? It connects people to Dave as a speaker—as a parent who happens to be speaking to them—and it sets the stage for him to make some powerful points.

You may not feel comfortable telling personal stories, but even still, you should tell stories of some kind. As humans, we are wired for stories. It's how we think and learn and remember. They are essential to making meaning of our lives.

So with this idea of needing to tell stories, let's imagine you are tapped to give a talk about mindfulness. You've seen the benefit of it for yourself and your clients, so you have the passion and expertise to talk about it. You know you want each individual to embrace mindfulness and make it a regular part of their lives because you can testify to the emotional and cognitive payoffs of it. So as you begin to lay out this presentation, you know you want to include a description of mindfulness and how it works, along with the way it helps people in their lives. You also want to walk the audience through a five-minute mindfulness exercise. When the evening comes to give the talk, you are ready, and you deliver it with confidence. From a technical standpoint, it was nearly flawless. But from an emotional standpoint, it just seemed to fall flat. You imagined it would really stir people, but the audience, while attentive and polite, reacted as if they had just heard a talk about how to install a kitchen cabinet. It was good information, but it didn't excite them.

When you dissect the talk later, you realize it's got great content, but it's missing the power of stories. When you delivered it the first time, you said something like, "Many of my clients have seen remarkable improvements in their anxiety after they started using mindfulness regularly." The next time you give it, you say something like, "I was working with a young woman named Erica who had anxiety so crippling she couldn't even talk to her coworkers without getting to the edge of a panic attack. Any human interaction filled her with dread. And yet she very much desired connection with other people. So not only was she anxious, but her inability to build relationships with others left her feeling lonely and depressed. When we first started, she was told that mindfulness was a daily practice and a way of life and that she would have to practice it every day for a few weeks to get much benefit from it. At that point, she was so desperate, she was willing to do what it took to feel better. Four weeks after she started, she went out to dinner with two other women at her office. Within six weeks, she was going to the gym near her apartment complex and was talking to a guy in her yoga class. It wasn't a quick fix or a miracle, but mindfulness opened up a world of possibilities for her."

You hear the difference, of course. The first time you gave it, there was no story to hook onto. It was just a vague statement about how many people have seen remarkable improvements with it. But the second time, you had this quick story about Erica and you cared about her and you also wanted some of what she's having for yourself. Your story that took only a minute to tell helped your talk go from cold to compelling.

In addition to good storytelling, we can't stress how important it is to connect with your audience by having fun. Much of what is missing with talks given by mental health professionals is a sense of fun. This means showing a sense of humor and a bit of playfulness. Many of the best speakers in our practice are just fun to watch. They are funny and playful. We've learned a lot from them. Recently Dave spoke at a state conference and one of the participants came up to him at a break and said, "You seem like you are having fun," to which he replied, "Very much." That's our hope for you, as well. We want you go beyond wishing you would rather be in the casket than on stage to thinking of your speaking opportunities as fun. Make that connection with your audience. Let loose and have fun.

To wrap up the talk, we would advise you to recap your main points in a very broad way and then give a suggestion for what to do with that information. It might look something like this: "Today I shared eight traits that are true of great parents. My hope is that it gives you comfort that you are doing some things very well. But I also hope it gives you some thoughts about how you can be even better at this very challenging job called parenting. Thanks for inviting me!" Again, like the opening advance organizer, it is simple, succinct, and leaves the audience with clear information to take away with them. So you want to tell them what you are going to say (advance organizer), tell them (content), then tell them what you told them (recap and summary).

This simple framework organizes your presentation in the minds of your listeners and helps them remember it later.

Even the Best Practice

One simple characteristic seems to separate the great public speakers from the others: They practice. A lot. Steve Jobs was widely regarded as one of the best business presenters in history. His talks and technique are widely studied in business schools. But Jobs never ever got up on the stage and tried to wing it. He put hours and hours of time into each announcement, each reveal, each talk. He didn't just put time into the content of his presentation, but the actual execution and delivery of the presentation. Just like our colleague Craig, he had it down to the minute. He committed it to memory. He walked through it multiple times.

Begin by asking the why questions. Why do I care, and why should the audience care? When you can answer that, move to laying out the presentation in a simple, clear way. When it comes time to deliver, focus on connecting with your audience by approaching it more as a conversation than a presentation. Think of it as the beginning of a relationship. And make sure you practice—a lot. If you do these things well, you'll become an outstanding speaker, you will serve your audience well, and you will help build your practice in some awesome ways.

eight

Lead Well

When Dave was in high school, a leadership expert came to speak to his class. He had written a book about the importance of developing strong leaders for the next generation. A few hundred of students were in the assembly while he strode around the stage imploring us to think of ourselves as leaders who were going to make an impact on the world. In the middle of his talk, he made a bold statement.

"All of you can be leaders," he said. "All of you," he said again for impact.

All of us can be leaders? Dave asked himself. *Surely not!*

He looked down the row and saw two guys, Allen and Dennis, sound asleep. Another couple at the end were giggling with each other.

All of us?

The speaker went on: "The challenges of leadership are enormous. Some of you might be frightened by the very thought of it, but every person in this auditorium can be a leader."

Over the years, we've heard variations of this "everyone's a leader in his or her own way" talk. The premise of this is that there are different styles of leadership, and people just need to find what style fits them best. Sometimes the idea even goes further and frames nearly every activity as a form of leadership.

Over the years, we have read more books than we can remember about leadership, most of them very good. There are some core elements to most of the good ones and a general consensus about what a leader is or does. We've come to the conclusion that not everyone is or could be a leader, or at least a good leader.

Here's our best analogy: If the athletic director of your high school stood before the student body and said, "Everyone here can be an athlete," would you agree or disagree? Well, we guess it depends on what he means. Is it possible that most everyone (with a few exceptions) can engage in some athletic activity? Yes, probably. But is it possible that everyone could be good at it? No, very unlikely.

Dave played baseball for eight years from the time he was 8 years old until he was 16. He went to practice, often started for games, and he worked hard. But, truth be told, he was probably a 50th percentile baseball player. On a good day, maybe 65th percentile. So was he an athlete? Yes. Was he a good athlete? Not especially. By contrast, his brother, Brian, was an exceptional baseball player and continues playing baseball into his 40s. Dave's son, Daniel, is an extraordinary three-sport athlete (soccer, rugby, and track) who is far and away one of the fastest runners in his school. His niece, Samantha, is an amazing volleyball player. Brian, Daniel, and Samantha are all good athletes. Dave is not. As much as he would like to be, he's not great at it. The issue is not whether everyone can be an athlete, but whether everyone can be a good athlete.

It's the same in most areas. Watch a few minutes of a reality singing competition and you'll be convinced not everyone can be a good singer, even if they really, really want it. Even with the desire, not everyone can be a great or even good artist, actor, writer, therapist, engineer, rodeo rider, bounty hunter, game show host, ventriloquist, oil tanker captain, storm chaser, herpetologist, roustabout, or hundreds of other things that require a mixture of unique skills.

And it's not just a matter of how much time you put into it. We said earlier that 10,000 hours is required to become an expert in something. That's true, but it's also true that we can't all be good at everything no matter how much we try and how much time we put into it. Dave has been driving nearly every day for 35 years, and he's still not a very good driver. His father has been driving for more than 55 years, and he's an even worse driver (though he has many other fine qualities!). Dave can point to more things that he is bad or mediocre at (being a handyman, shooting a basketball, fixing a car) than things he is good at doing. This is not low self-esteem, it's reality.

So the point here is obvious. Anyone can attempt leadership, but not everyone can be great at it. Like any complex skill set, it's not about whether someone can do the component parts of leadership, like delegating or communicating clearly or chairing a meeting, but whether these skills come together into a coherent package and can be expressed in an exceptional way. Let us use an example that baffles us still. Dave is a near-disaster at putting things together. His son's weight bench sat unfinished for the longest time because he couldn't figure out how to put it together, even with the step-by-step directions. Much to his embarrassment, he had to call another man to come over and finish the job. This bordered on humiliating because the whole time he's thinking, "I'm a decently smart and able-bodied man. I should be able to figure this out." But he couldn't. The same goes for household fixer-upper stuff. He's a disaster at it. Why? We couldn't tell you, but it's true.

Leadership is the same way. There are lots of men and women who would love to be great leaders, but despite their interest and even training, they aren't very good at it. There's considerable debate in the leadership field about whether leaders are born or made. We know the answer to that, and like a lot of things in psychology, it's somewhat complex. For many human traits, there is a certain amount of genetic heritability and a certain amount of circumstantial factors that lead to the development (or not) of a trait. For example, in the considerable happiness literature, it has become accepted that approximately 50% of a person's sense of happiness is determined by a biological set point. Some people have more inclination to be happy than others. It doesn't mean that someone can't become more happy, but it means that about half of subjective well-being is the hand you are dealt.

For leadership, the set point is about 32%, according to Dr. Richard Arvey and his colleagues who used studies of identical twins to calculate the variance (Arvey, Zhang, Avolio, & Krueger, 2007). That is, your genetics probably contribute to more than one third of your leadership ability. The other slices of the pie seem to be connected to upbringing, personal experiences, and early opportunities. This is encouraging, of course, because it means that much of leadership skill can be trained and developed. However, 32% is a whopping big chunk. In the extreme, this would mean that a person fully primed for leadership could get a 100 on a test and another poor soul with no leadership aptitude could only get a 68, despite good intentions and hard work. Arvey concluded, "It all comes down to the notion that there are some limitations in terms of who will or can become a leader based on their natural endowments." We would clarify that there are some limitations of who will or can become a *good* leader.

Organizations are full of people in leadership roles, but not all of them are well suited for their positions. It took us a full decade to figure out that not everyone is a good leader. It's seems so simple and obvious, but when you are part of an innovative organization that is committed to building brands and leaders, it isn't as obvious as it seems. Here's what we learned:

- Being extremely smart isn't sufficient for good leadership
- Being a decent person who is moral and kind isn't enough for good leadership
- Being a good manager isn't the same as being a good leader (more on this later)
- Wanting to be a good leader isn't enough to make you a good leader
- Having experience in leadership roles doesn't guarantee good leadership skills
- Thinking you are a good leader doesn't necessarily make you a good leader
- Owning a business doesn't make you a good leader
- Having good, creative ideas isn't adequate to make you a good leader
- Being highly skilled in a specialty area does not always lend itself to good leadership
- Exposure to leadership training doesn't always produce good leaders

So if these things don't cut it, what does make for a good leader? First, let's make a distinction between two broad styles of leadership: transactional leadership and transformational leadership. Pulitzer

Prize–winning historian James MacGregor Burns (1978) first conceptualized this distinction in his classic *Leadership*. According to Burns, transactional leadership, which is also known as managerial leadership, focuses on organizational processes, supervision of subordinates, and group performance. Transactional leaders are not looking to change the future. They are attempting to keep things the same but with greater efficiency and order. These individuals focus on good task performance, and they tend to use an exchange model in which workers get rewarded for good performance and punished for bad performance.

Transformational leadership, by contrast, is a style that enhances the motivation, morale, and performance of followers by connecting their sense of identity and self to the greater mission of the organization. Transformational leaders inspire and guide. They mentor and model. They encourage others to take greater ownership of their work, and they strive to understand the strengths and weaknesses of their individual followers so they can align each of them with tasks and roles that maximize their effectiveness. Transformational leadership is a style of leading that can create paradigm shifts and major changes through a ruthless pursuit of an organization's mission and larger vision.

According to Burns, these two types of leadership—transformational and transactional—are usually mutually exclusive. Although there is some overlap between good managers and good visionaries, of course, there are some significant differences in the way these two types of leaders think and operate. Here are a dozen contrasts:

- Transactional leaders manage subordinates, but transformational leaders develop a following.
- Transactional leaders tend to accept the status quo, but transformational leaders challenge it.
- Transactional leaders react to organizational change, but transformational leaders proactively create it.
- Transactional leadership uses carrots and sticks to motivate, but transformational leaders inspire through connection to the greater cause and a higher purpose.

- Transactional leaders appeal to workers' self-interest, but transformational leaders encourage others to put the group's interests ahead of their own.
- Transactional leaders emphasize correct and consistent behavior to improve performance, but transformational leaders promote creativity and innovation.
- Transactional leaders ask "How?" but transformational leaders ask "Why?"
- Transactional leaders focus on structures and systems, but a transformational leader focuses on people.
- Transactional leaders rely on positional authority, but transformational leaders have personal authority.
- Transactional leaders direct groups, but transformational leaders create teams.
- Transactional leaders emphasize control, but transformational leaders emphasize trust.
- Transactional leaders tend to focus on the short-term, but transformational leaders emphasize the long-term.

To be clear, we're not disparaging managers. Any good organization needs both managers who are the transactional leaders and the visionaries and nurturers who are transformational leaders. They both play indispensable roles and are essential to helping an organization function well. But sometimes managers are true leaders and sometimes they are not. It's not uncommon for people to see management and leadership as interchangeable. Certainly managers often lead and leaders often manage, but a manager is different from a transformational leader in some key ways. Those who are primarily wired to be managers tend to ask how to do something. We need a better scheduling system, so how do we find one, and how do we implement it? We need more space for groups, so how do we make that happen? We need a new receptionist, so how do we find one? For the manager, the focus is on taking an assumed question and figuring out how to answer it in the best way possible. By contrast, the leader asks "why" questions. Why are we doing what we are doing? Why do we need to do that just because everyone else is doing it or because it's just the way we've always done it? A transformational leader spends a great deal of time and mental energy asking why we do what we do.

Similarly, a manager assumes we need to maintain the current state of affairs. If a receptionist leaves, we need to replace that person. It is as simple as that. A manager allows for growth but uses the current template as the way to manage it. We have a lot more groups scheduled for the fall, so we need to find more space to run them—or maximize the current space. The way a manager thinks is that we need to figure out how to keep the machine running optimally. The transformational leader often begins with a challenge to the status quo. Why are we doing what we are doing? Why do we keep doing the same things? Whereas the manager says, "This is what we do," the leader says, "Why are we still doing things the same way?" That doesn't always mean it's good to stop doing what works or to do something different just because it's new, but it does mean the transformational leader tends to ask the disruptive questions.

And when it is time to make a change, the manager responds to the new demands and puts plans and processes in place to make it all work efficiently. This is an invaluable service to an organization. The leader may have thought it up and cast the vision for it, but the manager makes it work. A manager's overriding concern is how to set up structures and systems that serve the organization well. They want policies and procedures that make the place operate smoothly. It's not that they aren't concerned with people. In fact, many managers are kind and supportive. It's just that they approach their work with a focus on helping make the system run like a machine.

As we mentioned, one of the books that influenced us early on was Michael Gerber's (1985) *E-Myth Revisited*. In it, he says we need to think about setting up our companies like franchises. That is businesses that have regimented and systematic procedures that can be completed by anyone anywhere. The workers are trained to do their jobs in invariant, lockstep ways. So for a practice, it might look like having a series of steps that the checkout person does for each client. We've found this way of thinking to be immensely helpful for much of the operation of the practice, from intake to billing to appointment reminders to check-ins and checkouts. Much of the success of our business is due to having this consistent experience for clients. We also love Gerber's point that a little value-added touch in a business (let's say, being served a cup of coffee) actually becomes a liability when it isn't offered consistently.

To get to this good place of consistent and predictable, you must have good managers. You must have people who really enjoy and value making this big machine work. This is the emotional landscape and the mental territory of the manager. It's not that a leader doesn't want structures and systems. In fact, he or she probably knows they are needed to succeed. It's just that a true leader focuses more on people than procedures. The leader is more interested in inspiring and encouraging and equipping. The mission is to mentor and coach people to grasp the bigger mission and to move toward realizing it.

So when we are talking about transformational leadership, we are not discounting or denigrating the role of managers. However, we are saying that these are different things. You will have to have good managers to get to Gerber's ideal of the smoothly running machine, but you must have one or more transformational leaders to build your dream practice. That kind of leader may be you, but it may be someone else who is wired that way. These transformational leaders are rare. When you find them, you'll notice they are especially good at four component skill sets:

Inspirational Motivation—Transformational leaders develop and articulate a vision that inspires their followers. They challenge people to move out of their comfort zones, to explore uncharted, even dangerous territory. They connect followers to a sense of higher purpose that moves individuals and the entire organization forward. Transformational leaders not only have this vision, they are also able to articulate it in a way that makes it clear, precise, engaging, and powerful. Because of that, their followers are willing to go the extra mile, to sacrifice. They feel optimistic and believe in their own abilities like never before.

Individualized Consideration—Transformational leaders pay attention to each follower's needs. They act as a mentor or coach.

They generally respond with empathy and support. They keep communication and dialogue open. They celebrate individual differences and skills and strive not only to get the right people on the bus but to get the right people on the bus in the right seats.

Intellectual Stimulation—Transformational leaders stir followers to be innovative and creative. They encourage new ideas. They celebrate challenges to the status quo. They allow for experimentation and mistakes. The transformational leader doesn't just want people to make the widgets, they want people to invent new widgets or to come up with something better than the widgets. They create environments that are incubators for innovation.

Idealizing Influence—Transformational leaders are role models. They embody the values that the followers should be learning and acquiring. They not only lay out the mission and values, they live them out in a way that shows others how they can do the same. Transformational leaders have high personal integrity and are highly authentic individuals.

Each of these components is connected to the others, of course, but these four are the foundation of transformational leadership. Transformational leaders would give an enthusiastic "yes" to statements like the following:

- I naturally inspire others.
- I am good at creating a vision that others can get behind.
- I openly celebrate the unique talents and successes of my followers.
- I am highly tuned in to the personal needs of my followers.
- I nurture the talents and abilities of my followers.
- I am a natural mentor and coach.
- I challenge my followers to be innovative and do new things.
- I have an infectious enthusiasm and energy.
- I want my followers to question their basic assumptions.
- I inspire others to work as a team toward for a higher purpose.

So when we are talking about leadership, we're mostly talking about the transformational style. In *Leadership*, Burns writes, "Transformational leadership occurs when one or more persons engage with others in such a way that leaders and followers raise one another to higher levels of motivation and morality" (p. 164). If you consider what he is saying, it's actually really profound. He's saying that a transformational leader engages with his or her followers in a way that inspires them not only to work harder and better, but also to be better versions of themselves. By connecting followers to a higher purpose and a larger vision, a transformational leader helps these individuals work toward a greater good and embody the values embedded in the mission. That's pretty remarkable.

Dave admits that he is not good at many things. He can't hang a paper towel rack or dance especially well. He is bad at math and couldn't kick a field goal if he had to. He has a terrible sense of fashion, and he loses at poker. But for whatever reason, he's a good leader. Counting Southeast Psych, he has been in leadership roles in four organizations. In each case, Dave has been able to make some kind of visionary impact. We hope that doesn't sound arrogant. He is not good at most of what has made our organization a success, but he does have vision and an ability to get people connected to our mission and purpose. He has helped create an intentional culture that is built on our values of fun, innovation, relationships, and excellence. This is really his contribution to our dream practice.

Frank has also proven to be an especially effective leader. While Dave has contributed a lot of big picture vision, Frank has provided the inspiration, coaching, and mentoring better than anyone else. He takes care of our staff emotionally and relationally in some remarkable ways. He's funny and fun. He's aware of his own neurotic qualities and somehow manages to leverage all of them to be a highly effective leader. As he (sort of) jokingly says, "Dave's the 'dad' and I'm the 'mom' of the practice." He's the emotional, warm center of our family.

When we first started the practice, we made an especially effective team. Dave contributed a lot of the big picture vision, and Frank added the individualizing, nurturing aspects of strong leadership. We were both variations of transformational leaders. As we grew, though, we quickly realized neither of us was especially strong on or patient with the little details that were becoming more vitally important to our growth and future success. We needed more consistent policy and procedure; we needed systems and structures in place that would help guide us. Enter Jonathan Feather, who became our third partner and brought a mind and acumen for these details. He's a highly effective manager. When we decide on any big undertaking—adding a second location, moving the mothership to a bigger location, building a conference and group space—he's the man. We are convinced that we would not be where we are today without his help and contribution.

Here's the point: All of us have played an important part in the development and growth of the practice. Dave has been strong with shaping vision and culture. Frank has nurtured the individuals and gotten them more connected to the bigger purpose. Jonathan has helped us get the organization running effectively and efficiently. We needed each other. As we've grown, so has our leadership team, with each member bringing a unique perspective and skill set to the mix.

When Dave decided to step down as CEO, we were grateful Craig Pohlman, the director of our learning brand, Mind Matters, agreed to step into that role. Craig brings a big picture perspective but also has a mind for details and systems that is important at this stage of our growth.

For you to have a dream practice, especially one in which you are creating a group, you really need a visionary, a mentor, and a detail person. Sometimes that can be all rolled up in one person, but usually not. So as you think about what you want to accomplish, begin by doing an honest, relentless examination of yourself. Are you truly a transformational leader? If so, that's great. But if not, you can still build your dream practice. However, you may need to tap someone as a partner who has the ability to cast vision and get others to follow gladly and enthusiastically. Are you a great mentor and coach? If so, that's awesome. But if not, you need at least one other person who is. Are you good with details and managerial tasks? If so, good for you. But if not, find someone who's got that skill set.

Personality Traits of Transformational Leaders

We have known many people who truly aspired to be transformational leaders but couldn't pull it off. They went to trainings and read books, but they just didn't have the mojo to make it work. Some of them found themselves in positions of leadership, only to find that they were grinding their gears—and the gears of those around them—nearly all the time. This has fascinated and puzzled us over the years. How could someone who is bright, relationally skilled, and highly motivated to do well not be able to pull off effective leadership? How could someone read this chapter, for instance, and still not be able to become a transformational leader?

We are not sure that we completely understand it still, but we are getting closer to a solid understanding. We've come to see it through an analogy. When Dave was in college, he dated a girl who was a music major. She had a gorgeous voice. When Dave tried to sing, though, she would burst into fits of laughter.

"What?" he would say, fully aware of why she was laughing.

"Can't you hear yourself?" she would ask.

"No," he would say honestly.

"You're so off-key," she would say.

"Really?"

"Yeah, really. Can't you hear it?"

"No, I can't tell.

And that was the truth. He really couldn't tell. Today, his wife and kids laugh at him when he tries to sing, even when he is really trying to sing on-key. And he still can't tell! Truth be told, Dave loves music and wishes he could sing. If he had three genie wishes, this might be one of them. But, sadly, he can't. He is sure he could learn to be a better singer, though probably only slightly better. He will never ever have perfect pitch, unless he gets hit in the head with a brick in some kind of freak accident that will get reported in a psychological journal. The best he can hope for is to be a singer that people don't laugh at, and even that might be a stretch.

So, the analogy is obvious. Many people, including highly motivated and otherwise capable people, are tone deaf when it comes to leadership, at least of the transformational variety. As we've dug into what gives some people the intuitive grasp of transformational leadership and leaves others off-key, we've found some insight in the

Five Factor research. As you are probably aware, this model consists of the big five factors that are used to describe human personality. These factors appear to account for the different aspects of personality without overlapping on each other. There's a great deal of terrific research using the Five Factor model for many applications, as varied as parenting, learning styles, and even sports performance. With leadership, some of the research is contradictory and incomplete at this point, but a picture is beginning to emerge. Here's what we think we know:

Transformational leaders tend to rate high on Openness to Experience. This is so far one of the most consistent findings in the research. Of all the Five Factor traits, "Openness to Experience" seems to correlate the highest with transformational leadership. Those who rate high on this trait tend to enjoy new experiences. They love art and adventure and unusual ideas. They are curious and creative and highly imaginative. They prefer novelty over routine. It makes sense that this is perhaps one of the biggest predictors of transformational leadership. Because it is usually a well-integrated, consistent personality trait, it also helps explain why some people intuitively are so good at it and others are not.

Transformational leaders tend to rate high on Agreeableness. Those who are highly agreeable tend to be compassionate and cooperative. They trust others and are inclined to offer help. These people tend to score high on measures of empathy and generosity. Again, this makes perfect sense, based on everything we know about transformational leaders. Interestingly, there is some evidence that many successful entrepreneurs—not necessarily transformational leaders, although sometimes—actually score low on Agreeableness. They tend to be hardheaded, suspicious, and low in empathy. My guess is that these individuals are probably excellent businesspeople but not especially great leaders.

Transformational leaders tend to have moderate levels of Extraversion. They tend to be outgoing, but not overwhelmingly so. They connect with people and are energized by others, but they don't have to be the life of the party all of the time. Transformational leaders are probably a notch over the line toward Extraversion in that they can be gregarious and fun, but they aren't over the top.

Transformational leaders may score high or low in Conscientiousness. A transformational leader can be potentially high or low in conscientiousness. In other words, such a leader might be thorough, careful, organized, and even detail-oriented, but also might not be. Conscientiousness is a trait that is not necessarily tied to the ability to have a big vision and connect others to that higher purpose. Some great leaders might have it; others might not. It doesn't correlate especially positively or negatively with transformational leadership.

Transformational leaders might score high or low in Neuroticism. The findings here are definitely mixed and surprising. Although we wouldn't have guessed this, it makes sense that a transformational leader could be emotionally even-keeled or might actually be somewhat high in neuroticism. Frank admits he can be a tad neurotic. He can be anxious and moody and get stressed out easily. He tends to respond emotionally a lot of the time. But he's a highly effective transformational leader. The key difference here is that he is tuned into himself and his impact on others. He owns his behavior, and he is mindful of how he affects those around him. His neuroticism is actually part of his charm. He's hilariously funny and self-deprecating and almost painfully self-aware. So it makes sense. Putting this all together, the psychological portrait of a transformational leader is shaping up to be an individual who is extremely open to new experiences and highly interpersonally agreeable, perhaps mostly on the extraverted side. They may or may not be conscientious or neurotic.

This knowledge may help you assess yourself, as well as those on your team or even good prospects. Remember, even though many transformational leaders will probably rate high on openness and agreeableness, the reverse is not necessarily true. Those who rate high on openness and agreeableness are not necessarily going to be transformational leaders. However, assessing yourself and others along these lines can be helpful and a good start in the process.

We would add to this a few other traits that we can't necessarily support from research but have seen in practice over the years. A big characteristic that we have noticed in true transformational leaders is that they have a great deal of courage. They take risks and move into those uncharted, Blue Ocean territories. They also have a lot of moral courage. They stand up for what is right. They champion the under-dog or the unjustly accused. They get on the wrong side of argument when it's the right thing to do. We once read how one CEO often asks people, "What is one thing you strongly believe to be true that almost no one else agrees with?" Often the people who can answer this ques-tion directly are the transformational leaders.

We have also noticed these leaders are quick to accept responsi-bility and slow to place blame. They don't tend to make people feel defensive. Instead, they create an environment where it is okay to take chances, to stick your neck out, and make a few mistakes. When mis-takes are made, they are dealt with in direct ways.

Finally, we have seen how transformational leaders, although often big and bold, tend to be surprisingly humble. They can talk about themselves and their companies in glowing ways, but they are more about sharing their vision and their mission than they are about pro-moting themselves.

Building the Team

In addition to leaders, you will probably need other members of the team who serve the organization in either clinical or support roles. Every position in your organization, from CEO to intern, from office manager to filing clerk, is vitally important. Many organizations have sunk or been wounded by weak hiring decisions. Part of building your dream practice is building your dream team. You want individuals in all roles who line up with the vision of the practice and embody its values. You also want happy, fulfilled staff that are glad to come to work every day.

According to Gallup's State of the Global Workplace Report (2013), only 3 out of 10 of employees in United States are engaged in their jobs—and that's way higher than the rest of the world, where the average percent of worker engagement is 13%. We can only assume the reason for these abysmal numbers is that these workers are completely disconnected from the mission of the organization. They feel like they are a cog in a wheel rather than an integral part of an organization that is doing something important. You can help people feel important whether you are selling shoes or making electronics or running a practice. When Dave was CEO, he would sit down with our support staff once a month and tell them, "We are all part of something important, something bigger than ourselves. We are about getting psychology to people to enhance their lives. Each of us plays an important role in that." He would look at one of the staff members who did intakes and say, "When someone calls in, you are their first contact, their first impression. They are usually in distress or afraid, and they talk to you and feel safe and understood and supported. They believe you want to get them to the perfect therapist for them or their child." The staff would all nod with understanding, then Dave would gesture to the receptionist and say, "And when they come in, you are the first person they see and you are so kind and supportive, they feel instantly at ease." More nods. "And then they meet Diane in the waiting area who welcomes them and offers them a cup of coffee and makes them feel at home." And he would go all around and include the people who did billing and finances and kept the records in order and organized our groups. He ended with our checkout person and said, "And when they leave, you are the last impression, the last thing they remember. And they feel like you really want them to get the next appointment spot that works for them and that you really do want them to have a good rest of the day. And all of you, from the moment of initial inquiry until the time they leave our place, all of you contribute your part to making their lives better."

The truth is, he's not just saying it to make them feel good. He's saying it because it is true. The message is that we are all part of something big and cool and important and all of us have an important part to play in it.

You have to inspire well, but you also need to hire well. You are shaping a team that absolutely must be aligned with a bigger vision. You need people who understand that vision, can get excited about that vision, and can execute that vision. You also need people who have personalities that are a good match for the expressed values of the organization. Part of good leadership is making good hiring decisions.

A few years ago, we really needed another good child psychologist, and when we reviewed the applications, it came down to two people: a guy named Jeff from a prestigious Ivy League school and a woman named Dana from a school that was decent but nowhere close to being in the Ivy League. It wasn't Joe's Technical College & Tanning Salon, but it wasn't Harvard either. Not only had Jeff gone to the top-flight school, he had also scored an outstanding internship and postdoc. He had four published articles and was working on a book chapter. He was definitely a hotshot.

Dana, by contrast, had not published, had gone to a regional internship, and, at least on paper, did not sparkle nearly as brightly. That is, not until the interviews. In the interviews, she was fun and funny; she was creative and had tons of innovative ideas. She built rapport quickly with nearly everyone who spoke with her that day. She was also able to articulate a clear framework for how she approached therapy and gave really solid therapy success stories.

Jeff was reserved and withholding. He listened with a blank expression and rarely smiled. His answers were direct and clear, but, for lack of a better term, boring. After the formal interview, we all had lunch together (i.e., the unofficial interview), and Jeff smiled politely as we all joked and shared stories.

You already know where we are going with this. We hired Dana. Now, to be very clear, we are not anti–Ivy League. In fact, we have a whole swarm of them at our place. We've got psychologists who went to Brown and Princeton and Yale, and others who have gone to other top-flight universities. But the point here is that the best resume didn't get Jeff the job, at least not in our shop. For some other place, he would have been an absolute dream. For us, a fun and warm personality and goodness-of-fit trumps all.

We assume if someone has a degree from an accredited program that they have the requisite level of training to be considered for a job with us. At that point, it is more of a matter of how well they fit our culture and align with our mission and values. Dana was a great example of a good fit. She had a fun personality and a great sense of humor. She was creative and innovative. She connected and played well with others. And she did excellent work. She was the embodiment of FIRE—Fun, Innovation, Relationships, and Excellence.

Let us restate a point we've already made: We hired for *our* culture and values. We value fun and creativity, so we want to pick people who fit well into our culture. The culture and values in your dream practice will be different. Not better or worse, but different. As such, you should hire into your culture and values. And that's the deeper point. All hiring should be filtered through this lens. You have a mission you want to accomplish. You have values you want to embody. You have a culture you want to create. Every person you hire should be run though this grid. We certainly have plenty of Ivy Leaguers and people who have published. For example, our current CEO, Craig Pohlman, went to Brown and has published three books. But we hire people who fit well with us rather than people who have impressive vitas but don't square with our culture.

We have little turnover thanks to a stable clinical and support staff who love working at Southeast Psych. However, we have definitely made some hiring mistakes over years. We can count on one hand the number of clinicians we have had to let go. The main reason is not what you might expect. We have rarely ended someone's contract because of performance issues. However, we have ended contracts because a clinician was not a good cultural fit, even if they were doing well in their practice in terms of productivity. We've learned from both our successes and misfires in hiring.

Here are five things we've learned you always need to do when hiring anybody:

1. Always hire for goodness-of-fit with mission and values. The hire, whether he or she is a clinician or a member of the support staff, absolutely must be a good cultural fit. This is true across the board and without exception. There is a psychiatrist in our town (who shall remain very nameless) who has never gotten a good review from any of our clients. It's so bad, in fact, that we can't refer to him any longer. And the reason? It's not because he is incompetent or rude. It's not because his patients think he mishandles their cases. The reason? It's the receptionist. "She forgets what I just told her," one client said. "She doesn't seem to care about whether we get scheduled or not," said another. This receptionist is killing his practice, at least if our clients are any indication. And the fact that most of the good psychiatrists in town have waiting lists and he has none only supports this notion.

2. Always check references. As obvious as this is, it's amazing how often it doesn't happen. When we reflect on our hiring mistakes, nearly all of them involved a failure on our part to check references, for one reason or another. When you check, ask questions about the potential hire's personality, as well as his or her work ethic, contribution to the organization, and participation with group processes. Good candidates will get enthusiastic reviews; mediocre or poor candidates will not. References who are not forthcoming about the potential hire are giving you a wealth of information in their silence. The references should be glowing.

3. Always have multiple eyes on the candidate. Don't let just one or two people interview the potential hire. Instead, involve as many people as you can. When we were still running an APPIC internship (which we shut down only recently after our brains started melting from all the projects we had going on), we would typically get tons of applicants. We farmed the reviews out to several of our clinicians. From there, we would winnow the group down and invite about one dozen to one of two interview days. On those days, we made it a practice-wide event. Each candidate had half-hour interviews with at least two teams of two clinicians. They would also be part of a group presentation about the practice over lunch that involved nearly all of our clinicians. Following that, we would take them on a tour of the city in a rented van (where Frank conducted the most self-referential city tour ever; "Here's where my kids eat cheese pizza . . . and there's my dry cleaners . . . and there is where my wife takes yoga . . ."), and we capped it off with a cocktail hour at the home of one of our staff. Now, even though there were technically only two half-hour interviews (involving four clinicians), the entire day was really an interview. How did she interact with our staff? What was it like to be with him in a social event?

By the end of the exhausting day, we had a lot of data. The staff met on a later day to rank the candidates based on their experiences with them in a variety of settings and interactions. As a result, we tended to get some great folks who ended up staying with us well past the end of their internship.

4. Always take your time. Again, when we reflect on the times when we've bricked in the hiring process, it has been when we have felt some sense of urgency or need to rush. It might have been on the part of the candidate or some internal pressure that we felt the need to move it along quickly. Either way, the percentage of quick decision hires that turned out well is below the odds of getting a good fit when we took our time and did a thorough process.

5. Always give the candidate full disclosure. Not only do you want to get a good look at the person you are considering, you want that person to get a good look at you and your organization. Candidates need to get a sense of what it feels like to be part of this practice. Back to our intern interview day example, we constructed the day so we could get a decent read on the candidates but also so each of them could see how we interacted. The lunch presentation about the practice was basically our chance to mock each other, the city tour was basically an hour-long comedy routine by Frank, and the cocktail hour was usually just a free-for-all. Even with more seasoned clinicians, we do the same thing. We try to show our true colors so people know what they might be getting into. For some, it might be off-putting. If so, that's great to know quickly because it reduces chances of trouble down the road. For many, though, it convinces them this is where they want to be. Give people a good picture of what it will feel like to be part of your dream practice.

After you hire well, make sure you continue to inspire well. You want people to know your mission and values intimately. You want them to hear them repetitively, in meetings, in written communications, in presentations. You want each person to see how he or she is a piece of that bigger picture, a part of that higher purpose, an essential member of an important mission. This is the calling of the transformational leader.

Making Myths

Some people have called transformational leaders the "myth makers." These leaders are the ones who create the myth or story of the organization. If you read books about great companies that are written by their visionary founders, you realize they are creating the myth of that organization on the page in front of you. For example, in *Delivering Happiness: A Path to Profits, Passion, and Purpose,* Tony Hsieh (2013), the CEO of the shoe company, Zappos, tells the story of how his company has become one of the happiest places to work on earth. In his writing, he is creating the myth of that company. He is the storyteller who is shaping the Zappos narrative and sharing it with others. His storytelling shapes how we view Zappos from the outside, but his myth making also shapes how the employees see Zappos from the inside. When we say he is making a myth, we don't mean to say he is telling falsehoods. In fact, we bet every story and every example is exactly true. What we mean instead is that he is telling an idealized story that connects us to the history and purpose of the organization and inspires us to create our own.

We're doing the same thing here. We are creating the myth of Southeast Psych. If you were to come visit us, we think you'd find everything we've shared here has the ring of truth to it. We don't think we've lied or exaggerated, but we do think we are intentionally creating an idealized vision of ourselves to motivate you to dream big and move forward with courage.

We want you to start creating your own myth, your own story. We want you to have courage and take good risks. We want you to create your dream practice.

IV

Going for It

nine

Innovate Constantly

We share a weird phobia. We are both afraid of clowns. Deathly afraid. We actually both have T-shirts that say "Can't sleep . . . Clowns will eat me." We are afraid of circuses of all types too and will not go within a mile of them because that is where clowns live and breed (shudder). But, we would be willing to consider Cirque de Soleil, another kind of circus. In their book, *Blue Ocean Strategy*, W. Chan Kim and Renée Mauborgne (2005) describe a radical innovation in the circus industry. So radical, in fact, it might even entice us to join the circus.

The circus is a traditional model of entertainment. We want you to think about the circuses you have seen in the movies and visited as a child. Certain things were always true and present. At this circus you see a big tent, multiple shows or rings going on all at once including animal acts, concessions, and even an army of terrifying clowns. You can imagine it vividly. What would a circus be without tightrope walkers, elephants, people swinging through the air, and the guy with the top hat.

Based on your childhood stereotypes, you have an idea of what a circus is supposed to be. The circus industry has followed this model for more than a hundred years with nothing significantly changing.

Even without some of the traditional circus elements, *Blue Ocean Strategy* argues that Cirque du Soleil is still considered to be part of the circus industry. Cirque is entertainment but not a concert, a spectacle but not a ride, a story but not really a play. Guy Laliberté (the creator of Cirque) entered the circus space and blew up the whole idea of what a circus should be. Instead of three rings and multiple acts, entertainment consisted of one main themed act. Both Cirque du Soleil and the traditional circus have entertainers, announcers, acrobats, and concessions.

However, Cirque added a much higher production value and appealed to adults as well as kids. According to Kim and Mauborgne, Cirque was still fully within the circus industry, yet it essentially became its own new industry. This new space is described as a "Blue Ocean." Blue Ocean companies are still within an industry but are thinking about it in such a wide-open way that they tap into areas never considered before. This is the "Blue Ocean," and in such an ocean, there is no competition. It's there you can build your dream practice.

During and just after graduate school, Frank would try to imagine what it meant to be in private practice. He had never been to a psychologist and never knew one. But, just like with the circus, he had a pretty good idea what a psychologist's practice should look like.

As mentioned earlier, Frank's stereotype of a private practice was that of a quiet waiting area, a calming water feature, maybe some classical music, and awkward silences in a room with other "patients." This stereotype played out on television and on the big screen (Tony Soprano's psychiatrist, Robin Williams in *Good Will Hunting*, etc.). At one point in his life, Frank thought, "Now that would be cool to work in a place like that!" He didn't think such a setting could or should be any other way. Let's face it, people aren't usually looking for fun in a therapist's waiting area much less their office.

But why not?

Why is this stereotype still around? There are probably many reasons, but we think an important factor is that few psychologists have ever been encouraged to think about the "business" of psychology. Of course there is innovation in psychological research and theoretical schools of thought, but the actual delivery of psychology to the world seems to still fall within the realm of the office and the couch. The imagery of Freud, the couch, and psychoanalysis permeate the stereotype of a psychologist's private practice. Popular media has also promoted the stereotype of what a private practice should look like.

Clinicians, in general, have limited entrepreneurial exposure. They are typically trained to think a certain way about practices or the topic is never really discussed. In general, we are not encouraged to think outside the box.

In Frank's own training, he was taught to think inside the box and stick with standard practice. Although this is not a bad thing, the entrepreneurial business experience can be lost. We are psychologists in the helping profession, but we can also be innovative entrepreneurs who share a vision and passion for psychology.

Innovation in Our Dream Practice

By nature, Frank is an innovator. When working with dually diagnosed adults with severe cognitive deficits, he began to question why we did not bring these amazing individuals into our own world. While they had significant intellectual deficits and were sometimes nonverbal, why limit them? Why not help them find their own dream life. And so we went to Six Flags New Jersey with 12 individuals with IQs ranging from 65 all the way down to nonverbal.

Frank was close to one young man who was nonverbal, and as they were walking through the park, he pointed to the Batman Rollercoaster and was clearly excited. He thought, "Why not?" The eight other staff said, "Don't do it!" They had a mentality of limitation. Frank's was of permission and positivity.

We had a special pass, so this young man and Frank walked straight to the front of the line. The crowd looked at Frank in what to this day he interpreted (probably accurately) as shock and horror. As if he were dragging this poor nonverbal man around against his will. And how could he possibly handle a rollercoaster if he were so handicapped?

Admittedly Frank began to doubt himself, especially when the protective bars came down. The young man started yelling, but Frank knew it was just because he was excited. The watching crowd thought Frank was torturing the poor guy. They proceeded to scream their heads off and upon returning to the station, they jumped out with the young man yelling and screaming right back to the front of the line. He loved it! But the crowd around us just didn't get it. Frank questioned what was normal, pushed the boundary, and created a new roller-coaster fanatic.

At Southeast Psych, we asked a naïve question: "Why not turn the idea of a private practice upside down?" Why *not* question all the stereotypes? The Starbucks mission statement includes the phrase "to inspire and nurture the human spirit." The Starbucks mission is not "We sell expensive cups of coffee one cup at a time on every corner." Starbucks wanted to create an experience. By creating this experience, a Blue Ocean was created.

Always innovate. Innovation is the second letter in our FIRE acronym. Everyone understands this as a part of who we are, and it's so exciting to see people explore this side of their creative spirit. There are countless examples of this at the practice, including Noelle Bondy, one of our reception staff. She suggested we get rid of the check-in chairs and replace them with a built-in standing wall desk. This could offer people an easier space to fill out their paper work and also allowed for more freedom of movement as people came into our offices.

Another Blue Ocean thinker is Dr. Heather Wright. She began as one of our predoctoral interns, then became a postdoctoral fellow, and now is a fully licensed psychologist. Dr. Wright is building her dream practice in part due to her innovative spirit.

During her postdoctoral year, Heather asked if the practice could offer a knitting group to some of her clients. She suggested the knitting lessons be provided by our hostess, Diane Balcer and could be offered in our waiting area. This kind of innovative idea would never have occurred to me and actually threw me for a loop. Private practices don't do knitting groups.

We quickly snapped out of that stereotypical thinking and asked ourselves "Why couldn't we offer a knitting group?" Dr. Wright saw this as an opportunity to bring some of her older and more socially isolated clients together around a creative shared activity to build relationships and social support. No "therapy" was involved at all in this group, just friendship. And so, this knitting group has become exceptionally popular, and the life satisfaction of Dr. Wright's clients has gone through the roof.

How to Keep Innovating

We have visited a lot of therapist offices, and the prevailing model for practice development appears to be, "Let's recreate the traditional circus." A practice has looked a certain way for decades so why change anything? Of course people do not typically seek out a trip to a therapist's office to have fun, we say. People struggle with some very weighty issues in life and bring those struggles and trials into the waiting space. They just want to come to a place that offers some peace and quiet, not a bunch of fun.

That's our assumption, at least.

Just as Heather Wright questioned why we couldn't offer knitting classes in our waiting spaces, innovation begins with questioning everything. And also listening.

Innovative thinking can change the way you think about your private practice. And through this process, you can create a Blue Ocean practice of your own.

Earlier in this book, we discussed the process through which we named our dream practice Southeast Psych. It was an evolutionary process, and we learned a great deal about business, marketing, and, more importantly, questioning the status quo. The lessons learned have been translated into how we develop all of our brands. Southeast Psych is our umbrella brand. Within Southeast Psych we have a variety of "premium brands" including Rest Assured, Mind Over Body, Wise Minds, and several others.

These brands allow for subspecialties to enhance therapists' ability to build niche work and innovate. Our experience of building these brands allows for dream practices within our larger practice. Essentially, when a new brand is created, it's as if we are starting a whole new practice with its own mission and values.

Each time a brand is created, we try to follow the same process. This includes crafting a mission statement and developing core values.

Out of these discussions with team leaders and clinicians, we are recreating the process of building dream practices.

What's Your Mission?

You want to build your dream practice. We know this because why else would you be reading this book? Do you still really want to do this? You're still reading, so we guess that's a yes.

Why?

Tell us your purpose. Knowing the answer to this question helps guide everything and builds consistency into the culture and direction of your practice. If it isn't already abundantly clear, a great deal of thought and time should be dedicated into crafting your mission statement. "Getting psychology into the hands of as many people as possible to enhance their lives," is the mission of Southeast Psych. You're free to borrow it, but we doubt that's your mission.

Frank recently spoke with his good friend Ryan Kelly (coauthor of *Max Gamer: Aspie Superhero*) about future practice development. They were talking about Ryan's passion for fitness, life satisfaction, well-being, and so on. He is thinking through what his dream practice would look like, and one component included having a gym in the physical space of his practice.

Ask yourself how many times you have considered putting workout equipment in a psychologist's office.

Probably never. We know that we haven't.

But why not?

Start challenging old assumptions. Start innovating. Ryan knows what he is passionate about and has the skills to match that passion. He is thinking in a Blue Ocean manner. Part of his mission is about health and wellness within the whole person. Knowing that this is a portion of his mission opens up myriad therapeutic options for his future dream practice.

We could imagine a mission that goes something like this: "Whole Lives promotes living a full and balanced life emotionally, spiritually, and physically."

What a Blue Ocean that could be! We could imagine some pastoral care, elliptical equipment, a dietician, and maybe some corporate-based goal-setting groups geared to support a balance between work and home.

We hope you can see how the mission drives the direction of your dream practice but also opens up so many other possibilities. If you just stay stuck in the old way of thinking about how to do therapy, you remain within the stereotype.

Right now, jot down some notes about your passion. Don't think about what you do. Think about *why* you are in the helping profession. Be honest and be open to innovation in designing your mission statement. Explore your own mission statement without the box of old thinking of early training. Use Blue Ocean thinking. Brainstorm with colleagues and friends. Don't say no to ideas too soon. Hear them and explore them honestly and creatively.

Guiding Principles

As you recall, our core values create the acronym FIRE. These core values are our guiding principles. They are words and ideas that guide us and also allow us to ask questions that further our process of innovative thinking.

What qualities do you want your practice to represent? Do you want it to be cool, quiet, peaceful, exciting? It can be anything as long as it matches your mission, is relevant to your passion, and is economically viable.

Personally, Frank could not work in a calming and quiet private practice. It just does not match his style or personality. But he can easily imagine a practice where peace and stillness are core values. This book is about what you want your dream practice to be. It will probably look very different from ours.

Frank remembers the day Dave suggested, "I'm thinking for the practice, we ought to have a coffee bar." Frank's brain just went blank. As his Spidey Senses tingled, he knew something crazy or awesome just happened. Frank asked, "Why would we have a coffee bar in the practice? That doesn't make sense."

Dave furthered the idea by suggesting we have a group of conference rooms for free seminars and a book section for people to "get psychology." Frank really thought he was crazy. But the more Frank thought the idea through, it sounded like an amazing idea that fit our mission. Stereotypical thinking that shoots down innovative ideas is a hard habit to break.

We did all those things, but that was just the warmup. Later down the line, once we got clear that we wanted to push our message outside of our walls, we developed our "platform brands," the brands that allowed us to get psychology to as many people as possible. We started Hero House, our small in-house publishing house, and we overhauled our speaker's bureau and called it Super Speakers, celebrating each of our experts. But the biggest platform, in terms of money and effort, was the studio. When we walked the floor of the space we were considering outfitting and Dave showed us how much room it would take up, we all collectively gulped. But we knew we wanted—maybe needed—to do it.

So now this platform allows us to communicate the fun experience of being at our offices. From one of our viral videos called "The Flinch Test" that drew 180,000 hits in a couple of days to the more weighty topic of Asperger's and its exclusion from the *DSM-5*, our videos have allowed us to "get psychology into the hands of as many people as possible to enhance their lives."

One thing that keeps a dream practice vibrant and alive is to think of practice as an incubator of innovation. This incubator or "can-do" environment allows ideas to happen. It's just infused into the culture. Because of this, our clinicians, receptionists, and clients are all coming up with ideas. The members of your team will do the same for your practice if you give them the green light and create a culture where it is safe to think differently, safe to fail, and safe to dream. If it fits the mission of your dream practice and you have the ability to put enough financial and emotional resources behind it, then support it. In fact, don't just support it, go for it!

Arguably, innovation should be a core value of any dream practice. This chapter speaks to the core of challenging the stereotypes of private practice and how to engage society within the helping professions. You have committed to working within a helping profession, and we encourage you not to get stuck within the same old way of thinking that has dominated our profession for decades. Building a true mission statement that reflects your values and having core values that compliment your mission can move you in directions you never imagined.

So start your own circus. You may be surprised at what kind of crowd it draws.

ten

Build It and They Will Come

When we began to imagine our dream practice, it was an absolutely terrifying idea. Frank was 30 years old, and Dave was not much older (at least in dog years). We had little more than our movie therapist stereotypes, our stunning lack of business training, and a healthy dose of fear to prop us up. Not a lot to bank on.

Yes, we were terrified, but our bullets had already found a few targets in terms of fun and connections. Of course, we had a lot more bullets to fire, but we were already considering how to build our cannonball. We were passionate about helping others, and we knew we absolutely wanted to have fun. We could not work within the usual stereotype of private practice.

Borrowing against our homes and risking being our own bosses was not fun. In retrospect, that loan was the least expensive part of building our dream practice. We never could have imagined the amazing and rewarding relationships, experiences, and joys that have come from thinking about our work in radically new ways. But it took and still takes time and commitment to our mission and values.

We remember we would read through manuals from managed care companies and subscribe to "how to build your practice" newsletters. But we always felt they were somehow lacking what we needed and generally just restated the stereotypes. Specifics about getting loans, lease agreements, and other practicalities were easily discoverable, but figuring out how to build our dream practice was not as easy. We never really met or knew anyone who had done something different from the stereotype practice. Being in a Blue Ocean can be exciting but also a little lonely and scary.

The Setup

Every year, Geeks from around the world embark on a holy pilgrimage to San Diego, California. The pilgrimage is known as Comic-Con and is one of the largest conventions on the planet with more than 140,000 attendees in 2013. Comic book fans, movie stars, and gaming geeks descend on San Diego to celebrate their passion for pop culture, sci-fi, fantasy, and everything in between. Lego, LucasArts, Disney, and a host of other amazing companies are in attendance in force.

We have dreamed of attending the spectacle of Comic-Con. We have actually been on a waitlist for several years to get a table in the main hall to advertise the Max Gamer comic book series. But sadly we could never pull it all together.

And yet, in the summer of 2013, not only did we attend the convention, we had the honor of being professional panelists representing Southeast Psych. In our wildest dreams, we could never have imagined this trip. But our chance to go on this pilgrimage happened because of a culture, a mentoring relationship, connections, a niche, and innovation. Pay attention. All of the pieces come together in the end.

Piece 1: A Culture . . . and an Internship

From the movie posters of *Iron Man, Batman,* and *Wonder Woman* in our hallways, to the superhero caricatures of each of our clinicians, our dream practice exudes pop culture. In our dream practice, we promote strength and resilience through the theme of the hero. As far as we can tell, we are unique in that aspect within the world of private practices.

Through our décor, social media, and websites, we have unabashedly shared our sense of fun and innovation. Because relationships and connecting are critical to developing a dream practice, we pursued a variety of relationships with individuals locally and nationally. We also thought about ways we could reach younger clinicians before they became engrained with private practice stereotypes. But how could we reach them?

Through innovative thinking and brainstorming, our practice (without any graduate or medical school affiliations) created a fully accredited APPIC Internship site. It was our hope that through this program, we could share the model of dream practice development. We also hoped that in turn we could continue to be energized by youthful thought and creativity.

Piece 2: A Relationship

Enter stage right: Dr. Patrick O'Connor, the founder of Comicspedia. His website documents the themes in comic books. Think of the grief of Bruce Wayne (Batman) losing his parents or the alcoholism and exceptional giftedness of Tony Stark (Iron Man). Pat uses comics in therapy to help people overcome challenges in life and become better versions of themselves. Talk about innovation!

Pat contacted Southeast Psych for a postdoctoral fellowship after hearing about our APPIC internship site. Pat was seeking training and experience in how to build a private practice. He was intrigued by our hero themes and strength-based approach having learned about us online through our website and social media. He reached out to us as he felt his interest in comics, positive psychology, and fun matched our personality.

And he was right!

Dr. O'Connor completed his postdoc at Southeast Psych, and ultimately returned to his home state of Illinois to pursue a career in academics and private practice. In line with his passion, he currently teaches psychology students about the use of comics in therapy. Pat was also one of Frank's mentees through our mentoring program. They often discussed the need to fulfill a niche and build long-term relationships. Pat was passionate about psychology and his love of comics and shared this everywhere he could.

Pat made a name for himself and word spread through psychology circles and beyond. His reach was local and national in scope. Through his efforts to make a name for his work and passion, Patrick was contacted by Brett Culp, the director of *Legends of the Knight,* a documentary about Batman.

Yes. Batman.

Piece 3: Spend Some Money

At the time Brett connected with Southeast Psych, he was working on his own passion, *Legends of the Knight.* His film documents the story of Batman as a modern-day folktale. He tells how the story of Batman has inspired individuals to become bigger and better versions of themselves. The film includes stories of individuals overcoming trauma and physical differences. He even shares the story of a little boy who overcomes cancer using the identity of Batman as his inspiration and father figure.

Brett found out about Pat O'Connor during Pat's postdoctoral year at Southeast Psych. He wanted to talk about using Comicspedia in one of the segments of his film. When Brett came to our practice to film, Pat selflessly asked if Frank wanted to be interviewed.

Brett ultimately interviewed many of the clinicians in the practice. At the time, Frank was having fun and joking around with Brett acting like Batman and being weird. He was just having fun but wanted to build a fun relationship with Brett. He had no delusions about being in a film, but Brett was fun and Frank loved what he was trying to do. It was definitely a relationship he wanted to maintain.

Later in 2013, the trailer to *Legends of the Knight* was released. We were absolutely emotionally floored and stunned by the power of just the trailer alone. The rest of the country took notice as well through *USA Today* and the *Hollywood Reporter.*

After seeing the trailer, Frank approached the leadership of Southeast Psych and suggested we help fund the film and become executive producers. Frank approached Brett with the idea, and he graciously accepted. Our dream practice was now an executive producer for the film, *Legends of the Knight!* Because of that relationship, Southeast Psych, Frank, Dave, and Dr. Barrie Morganstein are seen in theaters and homes around the world.

But our story doesn't stop there.

Piece 4: Innovate and Connect

For years Frank had envisioned and dreamed of a comic for his young clients that would help them understand a variety of psychological issues. He imagined how these comics could present learning disabilities, trauma, anxiety, and Asperger's in a format that was fun, supportive, and exciting.

In 2009, a friend of Frank's and former intern, Ryan Kelly, whom we mentioned earlier, helped to develop and ultimately coauthored a comic book featuring a little boy with Asperger's. In *Max Gamer: Aspie Superhero*, Max uses Asperger's as his superpower and gains the love and acceptance of his sister. After a lot of hard work, Max Gamer, the Aspie comic book series, was born.

Because of Max Gamer, Frank met Josué Cardona, a therapist in Charlotte. They exchanged e-mails about his podcast, comics, and his take on therapy (www.geektherapy.com). They talked about how they might collaborate on future projects because they both shared a passion for geek culture, comics, and Asperger's.

Josué ultimately asked if Frank would do an interview with him on his podcast about his and Ryan's comic book, *Max Gamer*. They eventually worked out a time to meet up and do the interview. Frank connected to Josué immediately around our shared sci-fi and comic interests, and he was absolutely selfless in helping me promote his comic book.

Piece 5: The Grand Finale

In early 2013, Frank got a seemingly random "how's it going" e-mail from Josué. In the e-mail he stated that he had sent in an application for a presentation about comics and therapy with Pat O'Connor (they became friends and connected through their shared interests around comics and culture).

Frank had no idea what application he was talking about. He had to read the e-mail several times for it to actually sink in.

In the e-mail, Josué added that he actually included me and Dave on the application as presenters. He continued by stating that the application to present had been approved and included free four-day tickets to this "convention."

And to whom were we to present?

Comic-Con.

Yes. Comic-Con.

Not only were we going, we were professional presenters with free passes.

Frank nearly blacked out.

The application had been accepted, and he was hoping we would reply with a yes. Which of course we did.

And so we became panelists at Comic-Con and our dream practice was now an executive producer of the nationally distributed film, *Legends of the Knight*. At Comic-Con, many of the panelists, along with Brett, who had anchored a panel of his own, had dinner together. It was at this dinner that we were so stunned by the connections and relationships that had developed. Every major player in this chapter was at Comic-Con that week.

Because of these events, our dream practice gained a level of television, newspaper, and magazine coverage that we could never have imagined possible. And all the articles featured Southeast Psych prominently.

These amazing events happened because of authentic and deliberate relationships based on curiosity and a desire to serve. These relationships were tied to common interests and the niche(s) of our dream practice.

If we had set out to create all these relationships, it never would have happened. We needed to pursue our passions, build around our mission, and tie it altogether with core values and relationships that were authentic.

If we were generalists and tried to be everything to everyone, none of these amazing events or relationships would ever have existed. If we had stuck to the couch and hourly session model with a nice water feature in the waiting area, none of this would have happened.

This practice is our dream practice. We built it, and many people have been drawn to our vision. And we're still on this journey. There's much more ahead for us. New things to create and new ways to further our mission. Remember, our version of this dream does not have to be yours. There are so many versions of the dream practice. We merely offer this book as a way of thinking through the process to map to your own dream.

If you faithfully pursue the strategies and ideas in this book, your dreams might come true as well. You can have your dream job in your dream practice. In our practice, it's not about the superheroes, the caricatures, or the comic books. It's about the basics of relationships, connecting, innovating, and building an intentional culture.

Think about how you can communicate a genuine desire to serve others. This is our calling in the helping profession. But the underlying premise is that we are in the helping profession, not the "getting" profession. If humility and service is your calling and your drive, then the marketing, innovation, and relationship building will follow naturally. To build a dream practice, no matter the theme or mission, we believe that building authentic, consistent relationships is the key. This is true in friendship, relationships, and business.

Dream practices should be thriving all across the country, and we couldn't be more excited as we imagine all the possible versions of dream practices that could pop up as a result of this book. Through this process we believe you and therapists everywhere can transform the way the helping profession is perceived.

Please remember, you never know where relationships will go or lead. Whomever you meet, take that relationship seriously and know that it could take you in directions you could never imagine.

Often at Southeast Psych, we are on a wild ride that sometimes seems like it could go off the rails at any moment. But being unified and strengthened by a clear mission, values, and culture has made so much more possible than we could have ever dreamed. Fifteen years ago, we never imagined our practice would look like this or that we could share it with others to inspire them to build their own dream practices.

So now it's up to you.

Take risks.

Be bold.

Dream big.

References

Arvey, R. D., Zhang, Z., Avolio, B. J., & Krueger, R. F. (2007). Developmental and genetic determinants of leadership role occupancy. *Journal of Applied Psychology, 92,* 693–706.

Burns, J. M. (1978). *Leadership.* New York, NY: HarperCollins.

Collins, J. (2001). *Good to great: Why some companies make the leap . . . and others don't.* New York, NY: HarperCollins.

Collins, J., & Hansen, M. T. (2011). *Great by choice: Uncertainty, chaos, and luck: Why some thrive despite them all.* New York, NY: HarperCollins.

Dungy, T., with Whitaker, N. (2010). *The mentor leader: Secrets to building people and teams that win consistently.* Winter Park, FL: Tyndale House.

Gallup Organization. (2013). *State of the global workplace.* Washington, DC: Gallup.

Gerber, M. (2004). *E-myth revisited: Why most small businesses don't work and what to do about it.* New York, NY: HarperCollins

Gladwell, M. (2008). *Outliers: The story of success.* New York, NY: Little, Brown.

Godin, Seth (2009). *Purple cow, new edition: Transform your business by being remarkable.* New York, NY: Portfolio.

Grant, A. (2014). *Give and take: Why helping others drives our success.* New York, NY: Penguin.

Greene, J. (2008). *An abundance of Katherines.* New York, NY: Speak.

Heath, C., & Heath, D. (2007). *Made to stick: Why some ideas take hold and others come unstuck.* New York, NY: Random House.

Hepler, J., & Albarracin, D. (in press). Liking more means doing more: Dispositional attitudes predict patterns of general action. *Social Psychology.*

Jarvis, J. (2009). *What would Google do? Reverse engineering the fastest growing company in the history of the world.* New York, NY: HarperCollins.

Kim, W. C., & Mauborgne, R. (2005). *Blue ocean strategy: How to create uncontested market space and make competition irrelevant.* New York, NY: Harvard Business Review Press.

McLean, B. (2012). *Survey finds many living with mental illness go without treatment.* Retrieved April 10, 2014, from https://www.nami.org/Template.cfm?Section=top_story&template=/contentmanagement/contentdisplay.cfm&ContentID=1383 81&title=Survey%20Finds%20Many%20Living%20with%20 Mental%20Illness%20Go%20Without%20Treatment

Sinek, S. (2009). Simon Sinek: How great leaders inspire action. Retrieved from http://www.ted.com/talks/simon_sinek_how_great_leaders_inspire_action

About the Authors

Dave Verhaagen is a founding partner and the former CEO of Southeast Psych. He earned his PhD from the University of North Carolina—Chapel Hill and is nationally board-certified (American Board of Professional Psychology) in clinical child and adolescent psychology. He is a fellow of both the American Board of Clinical Psychology and the American Board of Child and Adolescent Psychology. Before starting Southeast Psych, he served as the clinical director of three mental health agencies. He is the author or coauthor of six other books, including *Therapy With Young Men* and *Parenting the Millennial Generation*. He and his wife, Ellen, have four teenage and young adult children, Daniel, Christy, Maddie, and Abbey.

Frank Gaskill cofounded Southeast Psych and currently serves as Director of Mentoring and Marketing. He earned his PhD from the University of North Carolina—Chapel Hill and previously served as a senior research psychologist for the Devereux Foundation's Institute of Clinical Training and Research. He is the coauthor of *Max Gamer*, a graphic novel about a boy with Asperger's who uses his special abilities to become a superhero. He and his wife, Liz, have two children, Olivia and Maddox.

CPSIA information can be obtained
at www.ICGtesting.com
Printed in the USA
LVOW10s2007050117

519875LV00002B/426/P